Sagittarius Surviving

Sagittarius Surviving

BY

CECIL LEWIS

LEO COOPER

LONDON

First published in Great Britain in 1991 by
Leo Cooper
190 Shaftesbury Avenue, London WC2H 8JL
an imprint of Pen & Sword Books Ltd.
47 Church Street, Barnsley, S. Yorks S70 2AS

A CIP catalogue record for this book is available from
The British Library

ISBN: 0-85052-448 2

Printed in Great Britain by
Billing & Sons Limited, Worcester

Contents

Preamble
1

Mediterranean Journey
14

Giro Classico
53

Into Greece
72

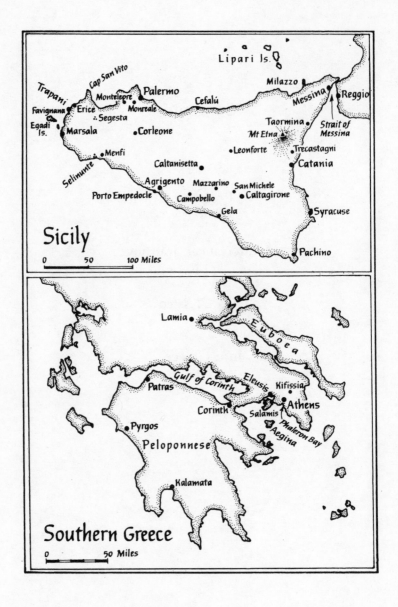

Sicily

0   50   100 Miles

Southern Greece

0   50 Miles

For O
From C
In 1943

Foreword

by Marshal of the Royal Air Force Sir Michael Beetham

Anyone who had the good fortune to read *Sagittarius Rising,* the author's autobiography of his experiences as a very young pilot in the Royal Flying Corps over the trenches in the First World War, will be fascinated to read this sequel of his experiences back in the Royal Air Force as one of the very few of that intrepid band who managed to fly operationally in the Second World War as well. So, for that matter, will anyone be fascinated who just reads this book for it is not only a graphic account of Cecil Lewis's wartime service in Sicily and in Greece, but also, in the form of letters written at the time to his wife, gives a series of cameos and travelogues which portray a vivid picture of the territories and the people there, both ours and theirs.

Cecil Lewis brings out the stresses and strains of separation and the human element of war suffering. He describes the frustrating problems the British Forces faced, having entered Greece as liberators, in dealing with armed resistance groups determined to take over from the legitimate Government.

How difficult it was, in the aftermath of war and enemy occupation, to bring stability to the country is forcefully brought home to us. They were desperate days for the Royal Air Force in Greece when they should have been enjoying the fruits of victory. It is a phase of the war not well covered by the historian and the author has made a significant contribution to that history.

I found it compelling reading and I hope you enjoy the book as much as I have done.

Preamble

Sometime during the spring of 1941 an Air Ministry Order appeared stating that any R.A.F. personnel who had once been pilots could apply to resume active flying duties — if they were medically fit and prepared to drop their rank.

At that time I was a Wing Commander, Staff Officer to Sir Philip Joubert, stationed at the Air Ministry. But I quickly decided that no desk job or rank tempted me to miss the old lure of the air. I made my application, passed my medical, reverted to Flying Officer and was sent down to Reading to learn to fly.

I had learned before, as some may remember. In 1915, at the age of 17, I went solo on a Maurice Longhorn at Brooklands after one and half hours tuition. Now, 25 years later, it took me one hour, twenty-five minutes to go solo in a Miles Magister. Flying is like riding a bicycle — once you have the knack you don't lose it.

After some further tuition, I was posted to Booker, a small country airfield in the hills above Marlow. There for a year, night and day, I taught boys, young enough to be my son, (including my own) how to fly.

But, by 1942 the shape of the War had changed and Transport Command was formed. There was a shortage of officers and I was posted overseas to Witney Straight's famous 212 Group which operated over the length of the Mediterranean from Casablanca to Bahrain.

The posting was the last thing I wanted. I was 44 years old, married to a beautiful brand new wife, doing a useful job and very reluctant to leave England for the rigours of 'active' service. But orders are orders. 'Join the R.A.F. and see the World' the posters used to say. During the next two years, I did so and collected a wealth of impressions and experiences that I have valued all my life.

These impressions and experiences are set down in hundreds of letters I wrote home to my wife. This book is an extract from them.

Plenty has been written about the beauties of Sicily, but nothing, I think, about the war period when I saw it and there are no records of the lamentable ELAS uprising in which I was concerned and which took place in Athens only a few months after the liberation of Greece in October, 1944.

This is not a collection of 'war' letters. Most of them have hardly any connection with the great campaigns in which England was engaged during those years. Transport Command, of which I was a member, was a 'servicing' command, a behind-the-lines organization, moving aircrew all over the world and ferrying aircraft from bases to the front line. The air terminals – then called Staging Posts — were charged with these duties and it was to command such a Staging Post that I was posted overseas just before Christmas, 1942.

Convoy

It was sometime during the night that the ship began to move and with the morning she was pitching heavily. The wind freshened with the day and the boys had to link arms at boat drill to keep from shooting over the deck. So far it was nothing but a good breeze with low cloud and poor visibility. We could see, right and left, a few companions of our convoy steaming in company with us and judge from their motion how little ours was, however much it seemed. The sea was deep blue and the crests foaming away from the ship's side with a boiling roar as they rose from under us gave that feeling of grandeur you only get in the deep ocean. There were heavy squalls of rain, the wind continued to freshen and by lunchtime fifty per cent of the ship's company were a good deal the worse for wear.

By now the great wind, getting up to gale force, had blown away the mists, the sun came out and lit the scene with metallic clarity. Now, for the first time, we could see what is, I suppose, one of the most majestic sights of these years. All round the horizon were ships: a great convoy had been called together from the ports of England and was now steaming in company. As far as the eye could reach, even when we were lifted on top of the rollers, were ships and ships and ships. Some close, heavy and matronly in their movements, some mere black silhouettes or smudges of smoke on the horizon, and among them went the little corvettes, seeming in the sunlight pale green, like lizards with red bellies, when they leapt from the waves and scuttled and twisted through them. Their motion was most violent. We could see their masts lurching from side to side, their bows go up and come crashing down, while we heavier ones only occasionally shipped a green one and rose from it snorting a veil of spray way back over the bridge and upper works. This great company of vessels was all moving together on pre-arranged courses and at constant speed, so that throughout the morning not a ship changed place. It was as if they were all attached by strings and were being pulled along together.

Today the storm is much worse. Either we have altered course or the wind has come abeam, for we are taking it broad on the starboard bow and as I write in the comparative calm of the cabin, I can hear the wind howling in the ventilators. Outside it is pretty well impossible to move about; the decks are wet with spray and we are rolling heavily. The seas are so enormous and so fierce is the wind that the ocean has a veil of spindrift over its surface and seems to steam with anger. It is an awesome sight, a full-blown winter gale in the Atlantic . . ..

The night has turned warm. There are a million stars in the

sky and a million twinkling points of phosphorescence glitter and wink along the sides of the ship and glow brightly in the scroll of the surf. Suddenly we are no longer in the north. All the men are leaning over the rails, singing quietly or talking in whispers, a little awed, I expect, by what will be to many of them the first breath of tropic weather. The screw throbs under us. The sea is calm. But the beauty of the night is somewhat marred by the rich odour of too many human beings who have been sleeping in their clothes for a week. No time to dress when you've been torpedoed!

There was a little impromptu concert given by the French contingent down in the lowest of the lower decks. Very hot. How well the French understand things of this kind. It was perfectly charming. The low girders across the bay, the army blankets for curtains, the men sitting in groups on forms and benches and tables, the cigarette smoke. The silly songs and stories, the excellent compère, the dancing, the accordions. There was one delicious song: *'Passant par Paris courtisant les belles'*, which had a haunting refrain: *'Le bon vin m'endort, l'amour me reveille encore'*. It was a happy hour, so much more intimate and friendly than our highly organized 'concert parties'. . .

It is Christmas Eve. The sun shines brightly on the Mediterranean blue. Ranges of mountains and blue hills rise into the clouds, the waves are white capped. It is warm and blessed to be in real sunshine again. Here are Moorish towers topping the mountain spurs, the relics of the Saracen in Africa. Here are olive groves and white houses fringing the shore, old fortresses with crenellated walls and ships coming and going over the water. The lovely day, the sight of land, the feeling that we are nearing journey's end has bucked everyone up. The morale is very high . . . All the day the sun has shone and with the evening more great battlements of cloud over Europe and the Orient turned to one huge rosy pearl. Then it all faded and the cloud masses went a delicate dove grey and the sky behind deep blue and the sea turned jet . . . I went to B's cabin for a drink of vodka - of all things! But, after all it is Christmas Eve though it looks like Midsummer night . . .

The Festive Season

Christmas Day was no time to arrive. It was cool and overcast when we docked. Algiers looked quite impressive from the sea. We were herded off the ship like cattle into an open lorry and driven — thirty officers all standing up! — some fifteen miles out — to this place. It is a scattered muddle of tents and huts. Quite pleasant I dare say in the summer, but on this chill Christmas dusk pretty inhospitable. We found camp beds and blankets (but no pillows), stone floor, running water about a hundred yards away, washing in the open, no utensils for meals, no light, nobody on duty. As darkness fell it started to rain!

Luckily I was with a couple of very good chaps. Neither of them had any eating irons so we all shared mine. We had tinned bully and turkey for our Christmas supper, tea, jam, marge and tangerines — all off the same plate — and the rain came down in torrents!

Soon the party began to get rowdy! We none of us fancied this, so we managed to slip away, sober. Coming back we got quite lost in the torrential darkness. After a lot of stumbling about we got to our tent and for about an hour various blasphemous and indecent remarks were to be heard rising above the drumming of the rain. At last, in the distance, a voice rose, a terrible, desperate wail: 'LET ME OUT!, it cried 'LET ME OUT!' It so exactly expressed our feelings that, of course, everyone roared with laughter. I shall never forget it . . .

Transit Camp

I have managed to get myself into this place, which is another transit camp — this time for aircrew. It is run by Transport Command, a cheap roadside estaminet — you know the kind of thing, one big room for bar and eating, bedrooms with loud wallpapers, tiled floors and french windows. Aircrews coming and going from all parts of the world stay here. Had I not seen the other conditions I should have considered this place pretty primitive. But I have been broken in and to be under a roof, have a room to yourself, a camp bed and CLEAN SHEETS! This is the Ritz!

I drove here this evening through miles of vines, now just dead sticks. It is not unlike California, rather brown in general, with palms and whitewashed houses in the Italian-Spanish style, red roofs, cypresses and far away the clean-cut line of the mountains, misty blue, hard dun folds in their flanks. But it has the scale of a Continent. I have seen the same sort of views in China, but Spain is the only country in Europe where the landscape is on such a scale. Aircraft wheeled coming in to land, there were American lorries and little Arab ponies and carts, miles of makeshift telephone wires, terrible roads, pools of mud after last night's rain. Everything that man had made was an abomination of desolation, but the majesty of the landscape remained.

Tonight over supper I talked with a Canadian, en route for England from Italy, having ferried a kite from the States, another from Cairo, another from Casablanca. The world seems to shrink as they speak. Remarks like 'I left my washing in India and shan't be able to get it till next week' gives the scale. But they live a dog's life, never seeing their base for weeks on end, living in a haversack, sleeping in their clothes, never getting a change or a bath, always dirty, always wanting — and rarely getting — their mail. They do this job as a rest from Ops and long to get back, for a rest, to Ops! It's a queer life and leaves them somehow nervy and drawn. The changes of temperature have a lot to do with it, I suppose. They may be sweating in the morning and freezing at night. Everybody — it's the first thing you notice out here — looks scruffy and dirty. Clothes are oily and muddy, boots uncleaned, people wear all varieties of kit (most of the RAF are in khaki), hands are never clean (I clipped my nails to the quick yesterday). It's pretty well impossible to get washing done. I felt sorry for these ferry types, doomed like spirits to wander for ever round the world. They don't ask for much after all — to have clean clothes and clean bodies and get their mail. It doesn't seem a lot, does it? But I assure you they none of them get it.

The White Knight

Jack got very high the last night in the other camp. When in this state he has very little control over his lower limbs. I took him back to the tent through the wood, supporting him as he tripped and swayed all the time, fell down, got up and lurched on again. He has a sweet character — you can always tell when a man is drunk — and kept up a monologue all the way: 'Never felt better in my life . . . The old school tie . . . Here we go, chaps... Steady . . . Never felt worse in my life . . . Any complaints . . . Everything under control . . . Never felt better in my life . . .' I thought if I could get his mind to work it might sober him up a bit, so, after his tenth fall, knowing he was in Flying Control, I asked him: 'How do you bring aircraft in now, on radio fixes?'

This stopped his monologue and he stood quite still for a moment, fixing me with a wavery eye. Then he lurched on again. 'It's a matter of imbuggerance to me,' he said.

Flight Into Egypt

You are a thousand miles away and by tomorrow night you will be two thousand, for I'm bidden to Cairo for an interview.

I know distance makes no difference, but somehow the actual geography of going further away from you depresses me . . .

I'm going in great luxury — in the largest airliner in the world

7

— it seats fifty-five people! With luck we shall touch down in Cairo an hour before New Year's Day!

Cairo

I had always longed to see Cairo, particularly the museums — which are now closed, of course. So far I'm very disappointed. It is all dreary and dusty, nothing fine or spacious about it.

The streets are full of soldiers of all countries, besides Arabs, Egyptians, Greeks, Syrians, Sudanese, a polyglot population which, since the war, has grown fat on the millions the troops have spent here. Over all is a smell, special to the place. Open spaces in the suburbs are squalid like the East, turbaned wretches sit in the dust moulding donkey turd into fuel or collecting broken glass, while the scavenging buzzards hover.

In Heliopolis there are fine villas and houses with clipped hedges and bougainvillaeas. They are flat roofed and, against the pale, pastel sky, have a certain beauty. But through these streets roam herds of mangy goats, driven by bedraggled bedouin who milk the ewes on your doorstep to save delivering the bottle!

Some men and women are fine and the Sudanese, black as night with their broad grins, are attractive. Sometimes the mixed blood comes out to give a carriage of personality and pride and even nobility, but mostly they are nondescript, fuzzy haired and verminous looking. I have also seen one or two striking looking women, but many who are monstrous. But even so they are better suited to this climate than our own women, whose white flaccid skins and strawy hair seem unhealthy and colourless.

Two Of A Trade

A real surprise today! I found out that Ivor is not up at Jerusalem, but on the other side of the Delta, doing his advanced training on Hurricanes! So I got the loan of a Fairchild and flew over. He was in the air when I arrived and when he came down I walked over and leaned against his Hurricane. 'That was a very ropey landing' I said. (It was). He stared at me for a full five seconds, unable to believe his eyes, for he naturally thought I was back in the UK. Then this incredulous fixed stare gave way to a shout of delight as he jumped out of the cockpit and embraced me and we walked off together chattering like magpies.

It is his twenty-first in a week's time and he is coming in to Cairo to celebrate. He is thin but fit and says he finds the work hard and tiring, but he is evidently doing all right and I am reasonably proud of him — and myself — for I think this is the only case of a father teaching his own son to fly, both in the RAF, and both flying . . .

When I saw the AOC this afternoon and told him I had been over to see my pilot son, he said, 'Your son!' incredulously, as if he didn't think I was old enough to have one! He is sending me to Sicily. I am thought very lucky for the place is within a few miles of Taormina, under the lee of Etna and is supposed to be an excellent posting. He is also letting me go out to the desert and convert onto Hurricanes and Spits! Wonderful! I always felt I was much too old for modern aircraft when I was back home, but here, I don't know what it is, but I feel full of energy and ability! Must be the climate!

The Pyramids

I went to the Nile Yacht Club to see if I could get a sail. The Commodore introduced me to two young ladies of the local Ministry of Information. They were jolly and friendly and when Ivor came in for his twenty-first (2 February), I was able to lay on a foursome. We went out to Mena House to dine and dance and see the Pyramids by moonlight! It was a real tourist excursion.

9

Mena House is huge and reminds me irresistibly of Bournemouth. One of those superior 'high class' hotels you may find on any south coast seaside resort — with exactly the same sort of people in it, only twenty years out of date — spinsters in feather boas, ruddy old colonels, dim, prim females with lace fichus, buxom girls at the puppy fat stage. The dining room is as big as a railway station, supported by bogus Byzantine arches, too many cedarwood screens, a sort of Turkish Tottenham Court Road effect, if you can imagine such a thing. It was all too, too pseudo and what with the discreet dinner orchestra and the superb palms and aspidistras we felt England was going native in a big way. The whole thing was rendered more paradoxical by the fact that the Pyramids were not a quarter of a mile away. In fact we went out after dinner to look at them — in a taxi! Really! All my illusions are going. It's too bad!

Dare I describe one of the Seven Wonders of the World from the top of which our late lamented Prince of Wales was photographed driving a golf ball? The desert in which they stand is higher than the road out of the Delta and so their incomparable majesty is added to by always having them above you. Their immense bulk does not seem obvious until you get right up against them. Then you have to put them in their background, the electric blue night sky, the arc lamp moon, bright enough to read by, the steady strong wind blowing over the desert as if the whole sky were in motion, the miles and miles of undulating silver sand, the timelessness of it all.

The shape which looks like the normal straight lines of a triangle from the distance — so huge is the bulk — is, when you get close, a series of gigantic steps each as high as a room, made from stones each weighing hundreds of tons. All this had to be brought from quarries up the Nile miles and miles away. But the manpower employed, the scale of the undertaking, which, even today, with every modern aid, would be considered well nigh impossible, doesn't strike you at first. You see the mighty line pointing at the stars, you see the huge flanks, the one bright yellow in the moonlight, the other dark mauve in the shadow, you get an impression of majesty, of immense age, of the inexorable crumbling of all man-made things . . . All this for one little room, no bigger than our cottage living room, one little room for one little body, one little king . . . 'My name is Ozymandias, King of Kings. Look on my works, ye mighty, and despair!' We stood for quite a time doing just that. Our minds somehow numbed by the grandeur and loneliness of the desert night.

Ostrich Eggs

This afternoon Ivor and I went to visit some early Coptic churches and the Crypt in one where the Holy Family is supposed to have stayed after the Flight Into Egypt. I felt this was rather like 'Queen Elizabeth slept here!' But one, called the Hanging Mosque, built on top of huge Roman towers, had some magnificent screens of inlaid ivory, ebony and cedar, lovely primitive ikons and before the altar large ostrich eggs suspended on chains.

When I asked the reason for this, the priest conducting us round told me the legend: the ostrich when she has laid her eggs does not sit on them but buries them in the sand. Then she crouches near them and gazes at them fixedly until they hatch. Should the female wish to rest, the male takes her place. The gaze of the ostrich exercises great influence on the unborn chicks and assists in bringing them to birth. As the bird, during all this time, looks neither to right nor left, but keeps her eyes fixed on the object of her desire, so should men and women do when they come to worship. The eggs are placed here as a reminder . . .

First Solo in a Hurry

Did my first solo on a Hurricane! There was quite a wind blowing and the sky was grey and gloomy. But during the last week I have done about eight hours solo on the Harvard, a beautiful aircraft, so well laid out that when I first got into the Hurry and saw the instruments, it looked like Heath Robinson, as if each had been added as an afterthought! However, I concentrated while the instructor gave me the dope about critical speeds and a few 'don'ts' and when he asked me if I would like to fly I said Yes, with a curious misgiving about it all. He didn't seem in the least bit interested! I initialled the 700, picked up my helmet and goggles and climbed in. Had I been sending an old gentleman of 45 off on solo in a Hurricane for the first time, I should have gone to the end of the runway, had the crash and fire tenders standing by and held thumbs! However, I suppose the way nobody bothered was a tribute to reports of my flying ability, my precious 2000 hours spread over 25 years!

The big engine opening up had quite a lift to it. I managed to keep straight on the runway and watched the boost gauge out of the corner of my eye. When it read -4 I stopped pushing the throttle open and lifted clear at 80. I held her down till she got up to about 120 and then started to get the undercart up. You see the pros whipping their undercarts up at 10 feet, but I wasn't going to hurry it the first time. Then the telltale lights showed that only one leg was up! This worried me. I thought I must be wandering round the sky like a flamingo, but there are two sets of lights and the second lot were okay. Both red lights came on. I sighed with relief! The next fight was to get the hood closed over my head. I managed this after a bit of a struggle and nearly getting my arm blown off! Then I throttled back to zero boost, set the pitch at about 2000 and settled down to stooge about a bit.

By this time I was up to 5000ft! Quite a change from the old Tiger! I then tried out the gliding angle, lowered my undercart and flaps, noticed the attitude of the aircraft so I wouldn't be low on my approach and make a 'creeper'. There were four other chaps in the circuit, so I had to wait my turn. It doesn't sound much and, of course it isn't except when you're nervy about your first landing! Mine was a humdinger! Not a bounce. There was plenty of time in the float and I found it quite easy. So I took off, and did three more landings and at last delivered the kite at the sheds intact. Funny how I feel quite up to this out here. I wouldn't have dreamed of tackling it when I was at home. Must be getting younger!

Bits And Pieces

Ivor's had quite a bad crash on his Hurry. He signed the 700 saying the tanks were full, but they weren't, so he ran out of petrol, forgot his reserve tank in the flap and spread the kite all over the desert. He's got two black eyes but otherwise seems okay. This is his second crash. I suppose he's due to have one more. I'm trying to wangle him an Italian posting. I don't fancy him in Burma . . .

Now I'm back in Cairo again. I've managed quite a bit in a week. I did eight hours on the Harvard, three in the Hurry and three on the Spit. The Spit handles beautifully, just like an over-grown Tiger! For my last trip I went over to see Ivor in the Spit! It shook him somewhat to find the Old Man ahead of him for he's still on Hurrys! I'll be sorry to see the last of him, but I know he'll do well.

Tailpiece

Last night I dined alone at the Auberge du Turf and found the following poem on the back of an envelope left on my table — by mistake, I presume!

> *Que faites vous dans mon lit, Marie?*
> *Que faites vous dans mon lit?*
> *Est-ce une espèce de chic chichi*
> *De vous habiller en deshabille?*

Cette confection en rose et gris
Serait très bien dans les Wagon Lits
Le dernier cri de boite de nuit,
Le mode de tout Paris!
Mais c'est plus pratique de mon avis
Si vous etes tout nue ici.
Permettez moi, je vous emprie.
Voila! Exquis! Merci!

Mediterranean Journey

I had a really thrilling journey. After spending the morning in the old bazaars (very picturesque, the only quiet place in the whole city!) where I bought a lovely piece of brocade for you, and getting some gen about Sicily in the afternoon, we took off sometime after midnight. No luxury this time. Only the empty belly of the old Dakota. However, I spread my bedroll and managed to get some sleep.

Cloudless dawn and nothing below but miles and miles of trackless desert. Over this the great battles had been fought — and nothing, but nothing, to show for it! Here and there the black dot of a burnt-out tank and then: First Stop — Marble Arch!* And there it was! Straddling a road from nowhere to nowhere! Commemorating nothing! A few huts, the airfield, breakfast primitive but plentiful off a brown tablecloth — no water here — and off again in forty minutes.

Miles and miles of sea this time. I got bored and read my book on Sicily. Then suddenly we were over Malta! What a sudden burst of beauty on midwinter day! I was quite unprepared for it. The tiny fields, all Devon red or bright grass green, were all outlined with white surrounding walls. This made a delicate pattern, a vivid patchwork quilt among which were low white clustering villages each with a high church dwarfing the little houses. Then Valletta, with its indented bays, its ships, its

---

*Erected by Mussolini on the border between Tripolitania and Cyrenaica.

15

white buildings, all looking so clean and tidy. The stone here is soft, cream in colour, you can saw it like wood, all the buildings are made from it. The whole place has a smart, cared-for look about it and, from the air, gives no sign whatever of all it has been through.

Another coffee and bun and we were off again and soon came in sight of Sicily. I got out my map and traced our course just off the coast. Pretty little towns in scalloped bays, aquamarine blue sea in the shallows, the perfect harbour of Syracuse, one of the famous places of the ancient world. Behind all the rising spurs of mountains. We bore away for Italy, seeing Etna's crater snow-capped above the cloud and soon sighted the toe.

This is rocky country, villages on mountain tops, broadening out to rich tableland, fertile, olive orchards, an impression of wealth. Mussolini has opened up the country with white straight roads. They say the best olive oil comes from this part of Italy. All very prosperous looking.

At last we came down at Bari. Thirteen hours in the air! I was all in. The Station Commander put me up for the night — on a stretcher, very narrow and cold. I was up again at five this morning, left at seven and landed here at ten. I am still a bit dazed, after a long exhausting day and trying to get hold of a host of impressions of this place and its people . . . There is an enormous lot to be done.

Herculaneum

Just back from Herculaneum! I was called over to see the Officer commanding my Wing, Group Captain Worrall, known to his cronies as the Baron! He is a most able and charming officer. All his chaps adore him and I think myself jolly lucky to have a C.O. I can respect — more than I can say for some I have served under!

We flew north over the Straits of Messina — the Scylla and Charybdis of old and saw Vesuvius smoking a bit. It's quite a second-rate mountain compared with my Etna! The Naples docks are a shambles, really frightful devastation, the worst I have seen. The Baron went out of his way to be charming and took me out to Herculaneum.

I'd always wanted to see this little place — reputed to be an artist's colony in the times of Pompeii. While it was a big flourishing town and, even now, as a deserted ruin, has a spaciousness about it, Herculaneum is tiny and confined. In the great eruption Pompeii was buried in lava dust, but Herculaneum was flooded with lava proper. The result is that Pompeii has been easy to excavate while Herculaneum has been a hell of a job — largely fostered by Mussolini. I was astonished at the small scale of it all, as I had been when I saw the Forum at Rome. Life for the private person of those days was very constricted. Houses were small, streets narrow. Only the Temples and Palaces were grandiose.

The domestic taste displayed at Herculaneum confirms my opinion that the Italians have none! It was all just as vulgar then as it is today! The tiny houses are built round a central courtyard, the roofs sloping inwards. So all the rain falls into a central pool. This gives character and privacy to the house. It is a charming arrangement. I had always imagined the town to be on a hillside, but actually, though now a mile from the sea, it was once on the waterfront; part of the quays have been excavated. On the way back we stopped and had a glass of Lacrimae Christi! Very good! What a name for a wine!

Coming back this morning we flew past Stromboli. It was erupting so violently that we made a detour to look at it. Rivers of white-hot lava were pouring down the mountainside straight into the sea. Hissing clouds of steam and sulphorous smoke rose into the sunshine. It was most impressive and I marvelled that peole are living on the island — two villages.

Then we crossed the Lipari Islands where the Italians keep their political prisoners and came low over Taormina, glimpsing the beautiful theatre as we passed by. Etna was snowcapped in a cloudless sky, she looked gigantic and very lovely. How lucky I am! This is an enchanted corner of the world.

South Seas

Today a young pilot brought over the Admiral from Malta in his 'barge' — a Beaufighter, painted bright blue! The boy was in the Naval Air Service and had been with a cruiser in the South Seas. He made me very sad with his stories of how Bora Bora has been ruined by the Americans with money and brothels, and Tahiti much the same. I suppose it is because I have such tender memories of those places that I hate the thought of their being commercialized and vulgarized.

Sometimes I despair of our civilization. The emphasis and interest are centred in all the wrong things, that is in material things not spiritual things. How right Shaw was to call ours the 'silly-clever' ages. But I suppose some will always wag their heads at the iniquity of the world. There was a Roman Emperor — Augustus, wasn't it? — who wished humanity had but a single head and he could cut it off! Even dear sentimental Barrie admitted that the greater part of mankind would be 'better dead' . . . We are a damned lot . . . I had a long talk with the boy from Malta. He was alive and intelligent, full of faith and hope for the future. I found him naive and rather touching. I hope he gets his world for he was one of those who deserved it.

The Opera

Yesterday evening I went to the Opera! Yes, we have an Opera House here — and it has escaped bombing. It was built in the 19th century, but in a style belonging more closely to the 18th and is really enchanting. Quite small, usual horseshoe shape, tiers upon tiers of boxes, big apron to the stage, a fine Royal Box, first floor centre, a painted ceiling with angels — which, as one of my pilots remarked were, in his opinion, aerodynamically unsound — any amount of gilding everywhere, angels holding torches, cupids holding garlands, columns, scrolls, etc, etc. In addition the whole place was lit with hundreds of white globes, no doubt once holding gas jets, but now electrified. When these were lowered before the curtain rose, it made a quite beautiful effect. But any time, this moment when the lights are lowered and the house is hushed before the curtain rises is, I think, the loveliest in the theatre.

The furniture was all covered with crimson velvet, there was a gorgeous foyer approached by curving staircases, simply dripping with cupids and angels which even overflowed on to the mirrors. In the centre hung a huge splendid chandelier. The whole place was well proportioned and in its own style quite perfect.

It should have been gay with an audience in hooped skirts, slim-waisted, tight-corsetted girls with high bosoms and low décolletés, lace mittens, ivory fans, coquetteries, and rippling laughter, each sentence beginning La, Sir! While the blades should have had their legs encased in tight trousers, worn side-whiskers, military tunics and Wellington boots and had their hair plastered down . . .

Last night, alas, there was nothing but dreary khaki, the ugliest of colours, a few indifferent women in moth-eaten fur coats, a few goofing children and very poor vermouth out of paper cups . . . The glory has departed in a big way.

The Liberators

After the show we went back to a neighbouring mess, where I left the company, much the worse for liquor, shooting crap at midnight. The amount of drinking out here is, I think, alarming. People seem to think of nothing but drink and getting drunk. These southern wines are pretty strong. We are not used to them and a glass or two has the desired effect.

But even more alarming is the amount of scrounging — a polite word for theft. An immense amount of this goes on, shamelessly committed by men who would never dream of behaving as they do here at home and would be outraged if they were committed and tried for it as they should be.

We allege that the democratic way is the better way and have come here to 'liberate' Europe from the horror of Nazism. But things are certainly worse here now than they were before we came and we seem to have no plan for bettering them. Sicilians never liked the Germans, but I think there is no doubt that here, at any rate, they behaved absolutely 'correctly'.

Our AMGOT* Government, which is shortly to take over here, is a joke. What can you expect? We arrive, turn out the administrators because of their Fascist tendencies. We turn out the seconds-in-command for the same reason. But then we have to stop, for someone must administrate, which leaves the third-rate people to run the place. Over them we put a variety of men, many of whom do not even speak the language, who have undergone a 'course' in civil administration of, I believe, six weeks! These well-meaning but utterly inexperienced officials are turned loose on the country. The result is bound to be amateur, bound to be inefficient, bound to flounder from error to error. The schools, as an example, are still using the Nazi books because there is nothing to replace them! The Brave New World! No doubt it will settle down in time, but the first impression of the liberators, in spite of the affection in which the population holds them, is distinctly disappointing.

I have given strict orders against this scrounging — and people can't think why. Everybody else does it, so why shouldn't they? We have fought for ideals and they are good ones, but it looks as if we remembered them best when we were near defeat and have forgotten them in victory. The 'aim' in the mind of the ordinary soldier is simply non-exist-

*Allied Military Government of Occupied Territory.

ent. He only wants to get by and get home. The important things are the mail, the boat, drink and women — in that order. My own officers are mostly men of my own age, mostly tired, like the men, by having been overseas too long.

I can see why men go wrong out here, why they drink so much, why they really don't care any more. For, if things go wrong at home, if a man is disappointed or betrayed — as so many of them are — there is absolutely nothing to live for. The job is dull, the war drags on, the people speak a foreign lingo he can't understand, a man has no one to open his heart to and there is nowhere to go . . .

And England who takes so much from her patient and loyal sons, what is she going to give them in return? Some guarantee of a better world . . . some hope, some greater richness or freedom of spirit? What will such men have when it's all over? A medal, some saving certificates and a few political speeches . . .

> O, western wind when wilt thou blow
> The small rain down can rain?
> Christ, if my love were in my arms
> And I in my bed again . . .

Syracuse

Yesterday was our first bad day. It blew a gale and was cold, with driving rain — and in this weather we went down to Syracuse. I wanted to put it off, but there were some vehicles to collect and as we needed them badly I decided to go.

We crossed the Catanian plain, where the heavy fighting took place just after the invasion, and came to the famous bridge where the glider boys made a great stand. The wreck of the glider they landed in is still there by the roadside!

I'd heard rumours that their attack hadn't gone too well. There was quite a lot of anti-aircraft fire as the gliders came in and the Dakotas that were doing the towing let them off the hook too far out to sea. So most of them couldn't make the rendezvous point. Some hardly made the beach, some landed in the sea and the boys, in full kit, had to swim for it. Not funny.

The wreck of the glider lying there looked somehow pathetic — all aeroplanes do when they're broken or crashed. Impossible that 'thing' could have sailed through the air and looked beautiful!

So much seems to have happened, but it's only five months ago! There were many burnt-out tanks and armoured cars, but now with the spring grass spurting through it is difficult to imagine the place as the scene of a battle.

The road started mounting, twisting through precipitous mountain gorges. We climbed through several mountain towns, poor and sordid under the rain, and after what seemed many miles over bad roads we came in sight of Syracuse. Then the rain stopped and the sun came out to cheer us. We found the vehicles we were looking for and while the men looked them over and readied them for the run back, I went off to look at the famous ruins.

The Greek Theatre

The theatre is at the back of the town looking down over the brimming harbour beyond. It is a beautiful position, quiet and detached. The auditorium has been cut out of natural lime-from the side of a low hill and the stone is soft enough to have preserved the ruts left by the chariot wheels leading to the Dress Circle two thousand five hundred years ago! The arches leading to the proscenium are intact on both sides. Only the columns of the stage itself are down. I wandered about a bit — there was no one whatever there — and sat down on one of the stone seats to try to put myself back into the age of Pythagoras, Archimedes and Diogenes. But I couldn't really get the feel of it, worrying, as usual, about getting back before dark, and so on. So I got up and went in search of the famous Sunken Gardens.

Apparently the Greeks always used to quarry their sandstone well below ground level and this made huge underground caves. In the great earthquake and eruption of 1693 — which wrecked Catania and most of the eastern side of the island — the roofs of these quarries fell in and the sunken gardens were created. The one I visited is now a lemon grove. Under one of the side walls are caves, some with lakes in them. Nearby I found men twisting grass into ropes with a very primitive wheel. They took me to the Ear of Dionysius which repeated my whispers back to me most distinctly!

Roman Amphitheatre

This isn't 500 yards from the Greek theatre, oval in form, like the Colosseum in Rome. It is in wonderful preservation. The arena is now covered with grass and in the centre is the pool where the gladiators used to wipe off the blood after their combats, still full of water! The tunnel round the barrier where the lions were kept is still there, even their feeding holes. At either end are broad ways coming down between the tiers of seats. Here came the great processions, the Emperors and Princes, also various 'turns' when performances were on. The seats reserving the ringside to the rich patricians were still there with their names beautifully carved in the marble. But the thing I had not realized was that, in addition to the combats, the slaying of the Christians, etc, they used to hold aquatic sports in these arenas. This one used to be filled to a depth of four feet from a neighbouring aqueduct, still in good repair, and then naval actions, water fetes and so on were held on this artificial lake.

The contrast between the two places was interesting, the Roman Amphitheatre looking in, the Greek Theatre looking out. I associated blood and persecution with Rome; with Greece Euripides and Sophocles. But how wonderful to see the two, in such a wonderful state of preservation so close to each other!

I came back refreshed in spite of the driving rain, forty miles in two hours over the dreadful roads.

Visitors

A sound of community singing comes up from the well of the hotel and through my window — which hasn't got any glass anyway — reminds me that a Squadron of Balts has descended on us tonight. They are a grand crowd and have that wonderful esprit de corps that you only get among those who are used to being in the face of death together. Over a hundred of them came in at dusk and the kitchens have been working overtime. This hotel used to have a staff of sixty in peacetime. We run it with fifteen and tonight we have fed over two hundred people! And we are sleeping them! Quite a different spirit is getting into the unit already. They are beginning to see that things can be better and are responding.

But it's a fight! My major engagements are not against the enemy, but against rival services. What I am asking for is the minimum necessary to feed aircraft up to the front line. It's a number one priority but do you think I can get it! I have to push, push, push! Most of the time I enjoy it, but by nightfall it sometimes gets me down. I wanted a station of my own to run! Well, boy, have I got it!

Saint's Day

Today, 7 February, was the Festa of St Agata, the patron saint of Catania. The main street — the only one of importance in this close stuffy little town — was densely crowded as the long procession came through.

First came men bearing a tall banner, then girls with another, singing, then Franciscan monks, then more clerics, and then — the Holy Relics. Two gold boots, a golden arm complete with hand and fingers raised in blessing, then novices, children and young monks in white surplices with purple fixings, all chanting and waving their fluttering white gloves before the image of St Agata which followed. She was the plainest possible type of German *hausfrau*, fat, round-faced, sheepish, crowned and decorated with hundreds of necklaces, seated on a sort of dais — being somewhat under lifesize — and carried by six or more men, groaning under her weight — for the old girl seemed pretty well solid gold and silver.

Every few minutes the procession halted, the novices sang, fluttering their gloves and the priests cried something which sounded like 'Madre Nostrum!' The population regarded this mechanical ecstasy with admirable sang froid. In fact when one of the officiating priests ordered those on the kerb to doff their hats, they did it quite perfunctorily, while the troops, heads covered, stared at the 'heathen idol' and probably made mental calculations as to her value.

This was the first time the Relics had been out since the war started and was the reason for all the excitement. The crowd joined the rear of the procession, a crowd that was really exciting, for here were the types resulting from conquest after conquest. The dark-skinned Saracen blood, the Spaniards, Normans, Franks, Huns, Greeks, Turks, bits of them were all here in the street. Some of the young men are splendid and the women can be striking, especially about the legs! I have yet to see a bad pair and the good ones are quite something! The priests also fascinated me; they were so exactly like the old pictures. Ascetic, skinny, pious, or pot-bellied, sweaty, bearded, cauliflower-nosed, pale and sinister, they might have been made up for it. Later I found the Holy Relics were in fact the limbs of St Agata. The golden boots encased her legs, the golden arm her arm. It is said that the flesh, centuries old, is still supple and living. I don't know why she was cut up. Anyway there she was providing a public holiday, a 'show' to impress the laity. It doesn't impress me, but nevertheless the Catholic Church remains the strongest force in Christendom and, on the whole, administers the most effective moral code to keep people on the straight and narrow.

Taormina

Countless orange and lemon groves flank the road from Catania north to Taormina. It runs along the coast with the Ionian Sea on your right. Although the day was grey and sunless, the fruit and leaves made a sort of golden haze beyond which the skirts of Etna rose, her head veiled in cloud. The earth here is black to dark chocolate, gashed with dry watercourses. A lava stream must once have flowed straight down into the sea. The gritty froth of it, curled and gutted clinker, gives a curiously gnarled and sombre aspect to the countryside, like no other I ever saw.

It is divided and subdivided into countless private orchards and terraces by high walls topped with tubular tiles which act as irrigation channels to carry water from field to field. Sluice gates of flat tiles cut or free the flow and, in the smarter properties, these runnels have been whitewashed so you can follow the course of the water. The overall feeling is of bursting fertility, with the black sticks of the vines already spurting their green spring fire . . .

Taormina is, as you know, one of the world's beauty spots. It stands about a thousand feet up above a bay between two rocky spurs, its houses stepped up along the precipitous mountain side. The road twists in furious S-bends. Mimosa splashes the hills. The gardens are all 'hanging gardens', the roof of one place making the terrace of the one above. It is clearly rich, well kept and prosperous, studded with hotels and pensions, all of which look out on the superb slopes of Etna which towers above it all.

We went to visit the famous theatre, quite different from Syracuse, chiefly because it is, surprisingly, all built of red brick! Somehow one doesn't associate brick with ancient architecture, yet the Romans did quite a lot of their building in it. In these climates brick does not weather as it does at home. I remember refusing to believe that the Frari church in Venice was old, the brick looked quite new, like something built yesterday.

The amphitheatre is superbly set, carved out of the hillside, steeper than Syracuse, a perfect semicircle, with tyring rooms either side, a 'backing' to the stage in grey and purple marbles, now much broken down, but having, of course, the perfect backdrop of an enchanted countryside seen through it, made even more magical just now by the clustering clouds of white almond blossom.

The whole place, now quite empty of course, had a dreamlike peace and serenity about it and I think I was very lucky to have seen it almost as it might have been in its virginity, all those centuries ago.

Lime Kilns

Yesterday I went out to buy some quicklime for the building we are doing. We had bought some before, but the price was high. I thought we were being given short measure, so, as I didn't want the exchequer to be done, I decided to go and see for myself.

When the Germans left, they blew up most of the buildings at the airfield. But they didn't do it very well and, with a bit of ingenuity and local skill, I am reconstructing most of them.

Of course my speaking fluent Italian has an awful lot to do with almost everything we undertake. Employing local skills makes an enormous difference in getting people's co-operation and speeding up the work. There are plenty of good craftsmen here, waiting to be employed and we need to have decent weatherproof premises to work from.

We found the kiln on the outskirts of the town. Terrible road through poverty-striken slums, all mud and rubbish, the people going in rags, barefoot. It was all very squalid. When we came to the place, the kilns were a cluster of tumbledown hovels set between gashes in the lava fields, a lime-baking community. We went to several before we found one with lime ready to sell.

In the yard stood a corner hut, low, dark, like a pig-sty. Somewhere inside, darker still, was the oven. I was too tall to get in, and so was the owner, a small smiling man. Amid the white dust on the floor lay piles of this softish yellow stone, the quicklime. Little urchins, six or seven years old, went into the place with baskets almost as big as themselves, filled them with lumps of lime, hoisted them on to their diminutive shoulders and brought them out to a balance — a sort of prehistoric bar and weight. It was primitive, but seemed honest enough. The owner chalked up the number of baskets on the door.

While the boys loaded up the lime on to our tenders, the owner of the kiln, in his shirtsleeves, hat askew, suddenly, apropos of nothing, put his hand in his pocket and pulled out a dirty card and passed it to me.

'My son!'

It was a snap of a typical dark-haired boy, big bold eyes, quite a decent forehead, looking smart in his uniform.

'Killed. In Africa. Last year. My only son.'

He brought out other snaps. The boy at the wheel of his lorry, with his mother and so on. While I looked at them, he turned away, picked up a basket, muttering, *'La guerra! Ah, si, la guerra, la guerra!'*

I didn't know what to say. I handed him back the photos, took his hand and held it for a moment. Then we paid, distributed a few cigarettes, and drove away.

But I couldn't get the old man's face out of my mind. It is such a typical thing out here. You get talking with a man, ask him how long he's been overseas or something and, after a few moments, without fail, out comes his pocket book and photo. Usually it will be of his wife or sweetheart, a faded snap of some children on a lawn, a pram, a dog . . . But this is where his heart is, the symbol of his hope, the thing he longs for, or is proud of. Sometimes, like the old limeseller, it burns on, out of pride, when all the hope is gone . . . I find these tattered photos infinitely pathetic. They seem such a slender hold on life, yet they are all men have.

When the boys have been overseas a long time or are overdue for leave (as many are), 'hope deferred maketh the heart sick'. Already I know this queer sickness. It is an actual physical thing, a sort of nausea that grips me sometimes when I think of the long days ahead . . . Well, there's nothing to be done but work to end it all, the quicker to be together again.

Guitry's Mozart

Our local opera people are pretty enterprising, I must say. Last night they put on *The Barber of Seville!* It's a gay and witty piece full of nimble tunes with a plot that is nothing but a ridiculous intrigue to give the artists every chance to show off — which they did!

Our Barber had a splendid manly voice and Rosina was slim and naughty. The rest of the cast were only so-so, but they kept the pace going enough for us to imagine how it would be when played, as it should be, with a maximum of adroitness and wit.

It wanted someone like Guitry to direct it. Did you see his Mozart? I went to the first night with Ricketts. It was a perfect example of elegance and style and when, at the end of the second act, Yvonne Printemps sang the Letter Song and the curtain came down on her holding a high note, to go up again and find her still holding it, how we both leapt to our feet (as did everybody else) and clapped and cheered till we burst the seams of our white kid gloves! I still remember the words of that song. It was a perfect love letter:

> *Depuis ton depart, mon amour*
> *Depuis, hélas, des si longues jours*
> *Ma pensée ne te quitte pas.*
> *Porte-toi bien, travaille bien*
> *Et puis amuse toi, certainement,*

Mais je t'empris, quand tu m'écris,
Dis moi que tu t'ennuie enormement . . .
Depuis ton depart, mon amour,
Ma pensée ne te quitte pas.

Yvonne was at the height of her youth and beauty then and Guitry, it was said, so jealous of her that he locked her in her dressing room between the acts! (He had lost one wife already through being careless). However, dressing rooms do not a prison make nor stage doors a cage, for she eloped with Pierre Fresnay right out of the wings! And a bit later Noel Coward wrote Conversation Piece for them. Remember? 'I'll follow my secret heart . . .'

Hurricane Over Etna

I've scrounged a private Hurricane! Taken the cannon out and also the armour behind the seat — so she goes up like a lift and handles like a Tiger! This morning I thought I'd take a joyride up to have a look at Etna's crater!

From the ground the mountain fills the northern horizon. Today it had a shawl of white cloud round its shoulders through which the cone stuck up like a cocked hat in foam. A plume of bluish-white smoke trailed away from the crater. At 12,000 ft I was just level with the peak which looked magnificent above the floor of cloud, sparkling white under a dome of blue. The crater itself was just a rim holding a flat saucer full of black lava. This surprised me. I had always thought of it as being a funnel. A wisp of smoke, like wood smoke, seeped out of the saucer, otherwise it looked quite dead, as if you could walk across it if it wasn't too hot. The main plume belched from a spot outside the crater. I could see the yellow sulphur on the rocks and almost smell the fumes. I must say I flew round a bit gingerly, remembering that Vesuvius had just been in terrific eruption and that Etna was due to go up any day. It would be too silly to be brought down by a rock!

When I turned south the whole sweep of southern Sicily lay below me. Magnificent. I felt quite warm though it must have been well below freezing outside. Then I came lazily down and cruised along the coast past Taormina. It's marvellous to get in some flying. Real fresh air after days of heavy work.

I think Etna's the most perfect mountain in the world. I always thought that Fuji was better, after marvelling at the Hokusai drawings, but a pilot who came through and had climbed it as a boy, said Fuji had a nasty bump on one side never shown in the drawings. Jap propaganda obviously — even their mountains have to be tops!

Vesuvius In Eruption

I flew up to Naples, passed Vesuvius and talked to people who saw the eruption. They say it was superb. Belching clouds cauliflowering up to 20,000 ft, the whole area powdered with fine lava dust and cinders which, when they fell, white hot, on the wings of over 100 aircraft, punctured them and put them out of action! (That's why, I expect, you never saw the eruption reported in the press).

When I came by it was all over, but the whole area, hundreds of square miles, was grey and looked as if it wanted dusting. From the air you could see where the two great rivers of molten lava had flowed down. They slid like long black snakes through the valleys for miles. People said it was still too hot to walk on them. Threads of smoke rose from them here and there.

I talked with a driver who had been up trying to help evacuate people whose homes had been swallowed by the lava. He said it was awe-inspiring to see it creeping along swallowing whole villages whose homes stood in its path and leaving perhaps only the church campanile sticking up. He said the advancing stream made an ominous noise, like the shovelling of thousands of tons of coke. This was where the edges cooled and grated like clinker as the molten stream ground by. This scared me. I had never thought of the noise it would make. Later I went up and looked at it all. It was like acres of that chocolate rock I used to adore when such luxuries were to be had!

Easter Sunday

Early in the morning, while it was yet dark, a clear silvery bell started to ring from a church nearby. A second followed, ring ing very softly and urgently, like a heart alarmed, and then a big steady one, deep and mellow, joined in, beating three beats with a pause and then three beats again . . . Generally I do not find bells sympathetic, but these had such sweet tongues and, while I lay awake and listened, I remembered it was Easter Sun-day morning and the bells were ringing because Christ was risen and the world must know. The ringing stopped, paused as if in ecstacy, and began again. So it went on, the triple beat of the big bell insistent underneath. I felt it must be symbolic . . . 'And the third day He shall rise again . . .'

So, when the light came, I opened my Bible and read that miraculous passage in St John which begins 'But Mary stood without at the sepulchre weeping . . .' and ends in the low ejacu-lation 'Master!' It is, I think, the most moving passage in the New Testament, and I am glad I read it again today.

I remember when I was very young (twenty-two), living in Peking, I went to the Russian Church for the service held on the Eve of Easter Sunday. The whole congregation carried candles and, when the service was almost over, we were bidden to go out, while the choir sang, to search for the body of the Christ. So we filed out into the warm spring night, a procession lit with tiny flames and, after we had made a circuit of the church, came back to find the great door bolted. We knocked on it and the Priest opened it and stood there with the Cross in his hand. 'Christ is risen!' he said.

I was very young and impressionable then and the fairy tale symbolism of the ceremony, its simplicity and beauty, moved me deeply . . . Afterwards we came home, still carrying our candles and ate the coloured eggs and cut ourselves slices of sticky marzipanny cake and everybody kissed everybody else, saying 'Christ is risen!' and we danced and sang songs and life seemed free from all responsibility and care — and, of course quite endless — the way it does when you are very young . . .

Spring

Things are easing up a little. Up to now we've had the whole unit billeted in this stuffy old hotel in the middle of the town — all the men, all the officers and all the accommodation for the transit personnel who are always coming through, and for whom the place really exists. Of course it's frightfully over-crowded and insanitary and not good for any of us.

So now I've moved the men out into a sanitorium on the coast, quite near the airfield where they can swim and lead a summer life. They kicked a bit at the idea, but now they're set-tling in and are much happier and better off.

We can spread out a bit in the Hotel too, have decent offices, spring clean, rearrange the whole place and make it better all round.

The Sicilians I've had working on the airfield building have smartened that up considerably. They've got a special way of plastering here. I suppose it's something to do with the fine quality of the lime. They get a shining smooth polish on the walls. I've got a suite of offices now, all looking quite posh!

And spring is definitely on the way! I was walking out on the runway yesterday, inspecting some wrecked German aircraft that have been all shovelled up in one place. They lay tangled and burnt and broken, bits of them flapping in the breeze, very forlorn and useless. But then I suddenly stopped. The grass on which they lay was a lake of wild iris, a mauve sea of colour about four inches high! A black swastika rudder swayed over the top of it. It was like a surrealist painting!

Duties . . .

It's been a simply awful week. Streams of visitors, changes of policy, worries and troubles and entertaining. It never seems to let up and it's beginning to get us all down. I've had several officers in hospital with various complaints, all of which are really overwork. So I decided this was ridiculous and planned it so that everybody should have at least one day off per week, otherwise we shall all go round the bend . . .

I planned to take my own today, but instead six people arrived unannounced and I have had to entertain them all day. Tomorrow there's a reception at the General's and the next day more Important Persons . . . Now, as I write, another Important Person has arrived so I must go and dance attendance on him. I wish I had more social gifts . . . However, it's unavoidable and must be lived through so that the end may come more quickly . . . I've had a headache for two days. I feel I never want to meet anyone again . . . I want to live alone in the desert — with you . . .

. . . Pleasures

I went to the General's reception. It really should have been more romantic. A big palazzo up on the hill with a wonderful view over the town. A starlit night, a rising full moon, an outside dancing floor, fairy lights and lots of delicious things to eat.

The female element, however, left something to be desired. Mostly nurses. Excellent women, doing an excellent job. Good-hearted, really NICE English girls. You know the type. 'We're Kensington Girls, from Kensington Gore.' D'you remember that from one of the Ambassador revues? 'My father's a General. I HUNT.' It was Joyce Grenfell, wasn't it? 'I'm simply grand at imitating sheep.' Wonderful artist!

The Palazzo wasn't at all bad. Large rooms, hung with glass chandeliers, majolica tiled floors, so shiny they looked as if they were swimming with water. Beautiful flowers, Arum lilies and big sprays of almond blossom, mimosa with bobbles as big as marbles, like puffs of sunlight, and long leaves like eucalyptus hanging down . . .

As only senior officers were invited and the General was there, the party had, thank God, some style and decorum. People think me stuck up because I don't attend those awful parties that many units hold where getting drunk is the sole object of the exercise. I always remember Tolstoy's question: 'Why do men stupefy themselves?' We're all of us dumb enough when we're sober, but when we're drunk . . . my God!

Adriatic Ops.

I was just changing last night when there was a knock on the door and in walked Ivor! You can imagine how glad I was to see him. He was on his way up to his operational Squadron in the north, the Mecca of all his training. I should have been even more pleased were it not that his Squadron is doing about the most dangerous job going — firing rockets at flak-ships, barges, etc at sea level up and down the Yugoslav coast.

He seems pretty well and has had the third crash I prophesied. Two of his friends passed through a day or two ago and told me about it. They seemed to think it was all in the day's work, saying it was a good thing to have a few crashes; then you'd know what it felt like! But it seems this last crash was no fault of his — in fact he brought it off in classic style. A Glycol leak in a Spit radiator forced him down near Setif. He called Base, told them, pinpointed himself, chose a nice field, had his switches and petrol off in good time and made a model belly landing.

Heroes Coming Home

Yes, we are bombing and destroying much that is irreplaceable. The loss of the old things does not matter, provided the new world rising from the rubble is finer and nobler. May it prove to be so. But I have my doubts. Architecture, more than Art, reflects the life of the civilizations that create it. From the days of the Tudors down to early Victorian times, England has boasted an unbroken tradition of glorious architecture. From Hampton Court to the Haymarket Theatre, from Tudor cottage to the Regent's Park terraces, at every level, for every purpose of every size, a thousand unknown men have created a reflection of our way of life. There is nothing to be compared with it in variety and beauty. Other countries may vie with us in the grand manner, palaces, cathedrals and facades; but when it comes to the village, the rectory, the manor house, the mill, the life of the people, there is comfortable peace about it that is unique and irreplaceable.

It was not until the industrial revolution that we fell into sham Gothic and pretentious plaster, balanced, if that is the word, by the hideous squalor of the slums, blocks of flats and 'ribbon' development. Our desire for a better way of living reflects our instinctive longing for a better way of life, to throw off the juggernaut of so-called civilization, which we loathe but cannot escape. It makes a great deal of difference the sort of house we go out to work from. Just to live in a fine house refines.

So what about the glorious boys who have saved the country? What are they coming back to? Matchboxes along miles of arterial roads! Acres of prefabricated rabbit-hutches! And from the papers it seems even to get that is unlikely. If that is the best that can be done, isn't the whole thing one further proof, if further proof is needed, of the futility, waste and degradation of war? Of its fantastic stupidity! Stupidity, after all, is the most powerful of all forces.

Orange Groves

Yesterday I found myself at 4.30 pm with nothing in my IN tray! Unprecedented! Some order must at last be getting into the chaos, though I have hardly noticed it coming.

I thought I deserved an hour off, so I took the car and climbed out of the town up into the foothills of Etna. Spring is now in full spate and the countryside is lovely. There is still a lot of fruit in the orange groves, but the trees are white with blossom at the same time. I drove through waves of perfume. When I had climbed about a thousand feet over the twisty rocky roads, I pulled up at a place where I could look down the hillside to Catania and the sea beyond. Below were acres and acres of orange groves. People complain about the worthless laziness of the Sicilian peasant. But it obviously can't be true, for the labour of building these walls and terraces must have been terrific. It is still going on today as it has been for centuries.

The strange faults and twists in the old lava fields have resulted in wonderful patterns of odd-shaped terraces and the high walls and black earth seem to emphasize that mania for secrecy you seem to notice everywhere in Sicily. They always seem to be hiding. You can drive for miles between high walls, unable to see anything either side. The Sicilian is all eyes. He is forever watching and gossiping about other people's business. He would even like to keep his orange groves secret!

Between the terraces where the run of the ground is precipitous, tumbled outcrops of lava remain. These jut out and are overgrown with thickets of prickly pear which gives a wild aspect to the otherwise highly cultivated scene. Then, unexpected again, sticking up among groves are tall black chimneys. Seeing one I began to look for others. Then I saw them sticking up all over the place. What could they be? Watchtowers to keep birds or thieves away? They seemed too high and slender for that. So I stopped the next peasant and asked him. It turned out they were water towers. Apparently the irrigation system is highly elaborate. In addition to the runnels I had seen on the wall tops there are large catchment tanks and from these water is pumped up to the towers from which it flows out, carefully controlled and distributed. This is all Arab influence — they taught Europe how to organize their agriculture.

After the noise and bustle of the town it is wonderfully quiet up here. I had stopped the engine and just sat there. Then I suddenly became aware of a soft and delicate murmur rising from below. It was the chirp and twitter of thousands of birds among the trees, like the running of a brook over shingle, a gay, smooth sound, hardly disturbing the silence. I sat for some time in a daydream and then came down to the busy smelly streets, much refreshed by the pause and the peace.

Pupi

In the evening I went with another officer to see the 'Pupi'. They are the Sicilian marionettes, of which the type developed in Palermo, the capital of Sicily, is world-famous. At intervals you may see them in London at places like the Scala Theatre.

The Palermo marionette is small, hardly more than two feet tall. But the Catanian type — and I believe those in other parts of Sicily — is a much more primitive affair. The doll is four feet tall, largely controlled by an iron rod coming out of the top of its head. There is usually a string to control the right arm, and that's all. The whole thing is far more crude.

After wandering about for quite some time we at last found the 'theatre'. Everyone wanted to know why we wanted to see the Pupi. They are considered rather like Punch and Judy, something only for children. When we got there — in a real squalid slum of the town — it was the most primitive 'fleapit' I ever saw. At the door sat an old woman with some coppers in a saucer. This was the 'box office'. Of course the owner refused to take any money from us, knowing, no doubt, he would get far more as a tip than he could ever expect for his seats. He offered to show us round and led the way 'behind the scenes'. The 'house' was nothing but a tall barn, with a tatty diminutive 'stage' at one end, some plain wooden benches for 'stalls' and a 'circle' above with a few stools where we were given seats later.

But back stage it was fascinating. There was a wardrobe of about 150 dolls. They hung on rails, in rows. All were mediaeval. Proudly the old man showed his 'Orlando' — the 'lead' in this saga of legend and romance that goes on, WITHOUT REPETITION, for six months! Orlando was a knight in full armour, visor, cuirasse, gieves, sword, shield, plumed and helmetted — really fine. The face, carved from wood, was well modelled and noble. He really looked like my idea of a Tristram or a Sir Galahad.

The other dolls were less ornate, but there was an endless variety in armour and costume. Kings, courtiers, soldiers, servants and a few, rather po-faced, moth-eaten ladies. Even Rosalinda, I regret to say, was a cow. There were also 'familiars'. These were about half the size of the marionettes proper and followed their principals about, providing humour and comment on the action and avoiding the soliloquy by giving the principals somebody to talk to. It was all, of course, smelly, down at heel and worn out. The proprietor was not a man of artistic sensibility, he was simply making a living and the show was a family affair. I believe most marionette companies have come down to this.

I already knew the play was a serial and the subject an endless succession of battles, intrigues, murders and elopements, based on the Frankish invasion of Sicily in, I believe, the 13th or 14th centuries. Frederick, Orlando, Charlemagne, all figure in this traditional story and it is really remarkable how it has lasted right down to the present day. And is still going on, giving to all the children, and particularly the poorest children, an invaluable sense of their hi   . and tradition. (I found later that my

Sicilian 'society' friends had ony vaguely heard of the Pupi and never dreamed of going to see it.)

But how had this simple, old man remembered the story? What sort of a script had he got? How did all his family know their parts in this six-month serial? I asked him what was 'on' for this evening and could he show me a script? He produced half a sheet of paper, pinned up on the side of the stage! On it were scribbled a few sentences in Sicilian. That was all. It was the briefest possible outline of the 'action' for that night. Evidently the manipulators improvised the action and the dialogue as they went along. The tradition must have been handed down from father to son for generations. They certainly had it all off pat. During the performance it all went as smoothly as if every detail had been rehearsed.

The children swarmed everywhere, up on to the stage, shouting, laughing. A fiddle, guitar and cello scraped away in one corner, the curtain was snatched up and the show was on. The knights swung about the stage making broad heroic gestures, clashed their swords against their shields, the operator stamping his feet to accent the words. Scene followed scene. The audience paid only casual attention. They talked, quarrelled, had free fights – which stopped the show until they were settled. Then it went on where it had broken off. The dialogue was all rolled out in a sort of singsong, half Sicilian, half Italian. It went on for ever. We stayed till Orlando had got his Rosalinda and then went home, quite stimulated by our extraordinary evening.

Of course it's all moribund artistically, but it only wants someone with a sense of the tradition to bring it all alive again and then it could draw the town. I heard that every Sicilian village has its Pupi. Perhaps that's an exaggeration, but clearly the thing is a tradition with deep, deep roots. If you ever go, take plenty of DDT! My, were we bitten!

Airing The Saints

This morning, my first day off for three weeks, I went with the family Russo to visit a small hill town which was having its annual fiesta. It was a perfect May morning and we wound up the hillsides I have described to you and came out on the uplands where pimple craters some hundred feet high have popped out like boils on the flanks of the great mountain.

The village we were bound for is called Tre Castagne — Three Chestnut Trees — and it houses three Saints, Cirino, Alfio and Filadelpho, who are housed in the village church and are brought out once a year to be paraded through the streets of the little town. This was the day and as we came up through the vineyards, seeing the town above us crowning the ridge, we passed many parties on the road, all going up for the fiesta. We got there to find the streets full of gay people milling round the stalls where lemons, oranges and strings of garlic were on sale. Everybody was dressed in their best and the whole place was humming with excitement, dominated by the clashing and clanging of the bells. You could feel the undercurrent of emotion thrilling through all the people.

The Saints are kept under a canopy in the Church, a lovely old Norman place, huge and dignified, whitewashed outside with corner pilasters and doorframes heavily carved with black lava and a noble, square tower above. At a given moment the doors are flung open, the bells go mad, the congregation shouts and screams with pleasure or ecstacy, according to the degree of their faith and, very slowly, a huge 'car' is wheeled out into the sunlight.

The Three Saints, just under life size, are seated under a canopy on top of the car. They are dressed in green velvet and armour and hold feathers in their hands, looking like a cross between knights and dolls, not at all holy. A narrow platform runs round outside their dais and on this two priests swing censers and sell favours — for the Catholic Church is an efficiently organized commercial institution and never misses the chance of turning religious fervour into hard cash!

Fifty people drag the car by its huge varnished shafts and fifty more check it on the steep hills by ropes from behind. Every few yards it stops for the public to adore and the priests to effect their sales and then moves on again. We pushed our way through the crowd to try to get up to it and the priests seemed delighted for us to take photographs and shooed people away so that we could get a better view. We purchased a small card with a picture of the Three Saints on one side and a prayer on the other. How magnificent the language is, how it rolls off the tongue: 'O martiri gloriosi della fede. Hoi exultiamo di santa goia ripensando i vostri immortali trionfi, che riportasti nei piu aspri tormenti.'

The whole scene was very informal and friendly. It was more like Hampstead Heath than a regligious procession. I saw no marks of devotion or awe, no cripples throwing away their crutches or falling on their knees to sing 'Sagittas' as they do at Seville. It was all gay, sunlight and bells, and happy people cheering the saints.

We then retired to the beautiful old house belonging to Russo's friends, walked up a stairway on to a terrace and so stood looking down on the crowd below where the procession was going by. The finest lemons are now in season. They are as big as grapefruit, not at all bitter and you eat not the flesh but the inner white rind, which is thick and soft. It was very cool and refreshing after the hot stuffy crowd and when they had all passed by I turned round and was astounded by the view.

The town stands about 3000ft up on a ridge. Above lies the ballet skirt of Etna, a superb cone of glistening white, ineffable in its serenity and purity. Below, looking over the roof of the old house, miles and miles of vineyards swing down to the Ionian Sea. Everywhere the vines climb, overflowing right on to the terrace of the house, everywhere they wave their thin spring tendrils on which next year's wine now stands erect in tiny clusters, each infant grape no bigger than a pin's head. The profusion of it all in that setting quite overwhelmed me. The vine seemed the very incarnation of eternal life! Its fruit the distillation of sunlight, its juice the elixir and consolation to the heart of man! I knew then why Sicily has been called the Garden of the Mediterranean. You could almost hear the sap rising and throbbing in the warm stems as the blessed tides of life welled back to our war-weary world.

We then went back into the shady house to drink some of this elixir. It was clear amber in colour, tasted slightly smokey and was strong enough for me to feel a bit squiffy. So did the Signora. She said she felt quite 'tinned' which I at last understood to be her attempt to talk slang and was to be translated as 'canned'. She speaks quite good English, to which these occasional lapses add flavour.

Laundry

Today at last I got the Laundry set up. Set up and working. I am really quite proud of it. Remember how I wrote to you when I was stuck in that RAF Transit Camp near Algiers and met all those ferry pilots for the first time. They were really lost souls. Nobody was reponsible for them, or took care of them, saw to it that they were properly housed and fed. They were scruffy, smelly and I thought most of them were probably lousy as well. They stuck in my mind. I thought it was a scandal, but I couldn't do anything about it.

When I got here I did look after the rooms where we put up aircrew in transit through this place, saw that they had clean linen and pillows and light: but of course the real snag was their dirty linen. I couldn't do anything about that until I moved the men out to the airfield. That left us with lots more space and when we got it all cleaned up I found the Hotel had a flat tiled floor on the roof! The place had been used for laundry I believe before the war. And it took no time at all to get it serviceable.

But when we got down to it, we found the snags. The boys had no change of clothes! Maybe a shirt and a pair of socks at the most. They were usually only here for a night, and had to be away early next morning. That gave us eight hours. If they would trust us, give us all their dirty clothes and go to bed naked, I thought we could just make it. But we would have to work fast.

First we had to find the washerwomen. It turned out they were all scared stiff of going out at night and the idea of working through the night was something they'd never dreamed of. But luckily we found a local man who'd been in the laundry business before the war and he organized it, got the women, arranged how much they were to be paid and took on the responsibility of seeing they finished the job in time. Our own chaps on night duty at the hotel entrance had to see to collecting and delivering the washing to the right rooms. If that went wrong, we should never have any repeat orders!

I had a notice put up in the hall: 'Give your dirty linen to the Corporal on duty by 10 p.m. You will have it back by 6 a.m. clean and dry.' I signed this, as a sort of guarantee that nobody was on the make and tonight for the first time were open for business! I've financed it out of petty cash! I hope they'll wear it – and I hope we'll be a success. (Later. We were!)

Sicilian Carts

I was awakened by the sound of tambourines and ocarina music and went to the window to see the parade of Sicilian carts going by. They were done up to the nines for the occasion. The horses, richly caparisoned, halters, collars and cloths, were all embroidered in sequins and looked mediaeval. Tall plumes of pheasant feathers nodded from their heads and their yokes were crowned with ostrich plumes, like noble feather dusters.

The cart itself is painted all over, each panel a scene from the Middle Ages. The background colour is usually a pale lime green, sometimes a bright vermillion. In some carts the painting is really well done, the whole thing varnished and obviously kept with the greatest care and pride. Below the panels of the cart, a low square-sided affair, are stringers carved with a procession of saints and dignitaries in low relief. Axles and wheels are all painted. In some each spoke where it meets the rim has a small white dove carved in high relief. Underneath, where you can hardly see it, is a screen of delicate wrought iron work. I don't know why it is there or what purpose it serves, but I was charmed to see such workmanship so hidden. Craftsmanship is alive when the whole thing has to be perfect, not just what is seen.

Even some of the nosebags were embroidered all over with sequins and the owner of one cart shooed people away so we could see it clearly. He was obviously frightfully proud of it and sat with other men and a young girl in the cart for us to photograph it. All the time they kept up this gay simple music that repeated itself.

There were dozens of carts. Some had horses covered with nets all fluttering with bobbles and ribbons, others carried dozens of rosettes, one trotting car had nothing but one immense pheasant tail feather on the horse's head which bent in the wind as the cart rushed by. The whole scene was full of 'allegria', as they say, jingling, jangling, clattering hooves, shouting, whistling, clouds of dust and cheering crowds and over it all, sunlight and blue sky.

Whitney Straight

Just back from another Cairo conference with the AOC. From time to time he invites us down to Cairo to chew the rag and get the feel of how we're doing. I think it's a very good idea. Gives us a break, boosts morale and reminds us he's not a dyed in the wool 'service' officer, but has a really 'civilian' point of view, goes for what he wants, cuts the red tape, is very free and easy and at the same time earns and certainly gets our respect and devotion..

Some people say he's too quick off the mark and cuts too many corners. But people must have something to grumble about. They don't understand that if a man does the right thing fifty percent of the time, he's a good man.

What I personally admire is his loyalty to his staff, his generosity and understanding when a man gets into some trouble, usually overstepping service regulations or security and things like that. I've known men who would have been broken had the 'usual channels' been allowed to take their course. Whitney just used his prerogative to deal with the offence 'summarily', quashed the case, tore a strip off the chap over a drink and that was that. Men don't forget a thing like that and, of course, he gets wonderful co-operation and affection from everybody.

So we enjoyed the trip — though Cairo isn't what it was. The desert war is over. The front line is now over 500 miles away. It's all looking a bit more tatty than the last time I was down. Groppi's, the most famous cake shop in the Middle East, much patronized by officers who were sitting there on their backsides when the war was on and so came to be called Groppi's Light Horse, is now much the worse for wear!

The only thing that really cheered me was when I was shopping in the bazaars. I heard the sound of a drum and the piping of a flute and looked out to see what it was. The street was crowded and narrow and down it came the drummer and flautist making a merry noise. They were calling the attention of the populace to the goods that followed — a splendid young Arab stallion. He stepped so delicately and so proudly, long mane, tossing head, sleek white coat and seemed so confident of his powers, which as everyone could see were considerable, that I felt I should like to hire that little orchestra to precede me down the lane when I come home!

Hospitality

I was wakened last night around midnight by a knock on my door. Half asleep, I said 'Come in'. The door opened and there stood an Army Sergeant. He sprang to attention and saluted me smartly. Military Police, he told me, were in charge of law and order in the town, as far as it concerned all army personnel and did I know that 'my' hotel was being used as a brothel?

Extremely surprised at such an intrusion, I felt bound to confess, light-heartedly, that such a possibility had so far seemed too good to be true.

The Sergeant was not amused. He had 'removed' the tarts from the room, he explained, and two of his men were holding them down in the hall and would I, please, come down to verify the facts, see the women and investigate.

Reluctantly, I pulled on some clothes and went down. It seemed that the Corporal on night door duty had, earlier in the evening, given a key to three aircrew who said they would all like to sleep in the same room. There was nothing unusual in that, but later in the evening when he saw the three return, they had collected a couple of girls who, waist in waist, they were happily ushering upstairs.

The Corporal didn't know what to do. The aircrew were probably officers and he didn't know if he had the authority to stop them. He felt it was an offence, but how to deal with it? He was stumped. Just then it happened the Sergeant, Military Police, came by. He often dropped in to see if things were all right. The Corporal told him.

The Sergeant, furious, said such things were very far from all right, went straight up to the room and walked in.

'You wouldn't believe it, sir,' he told me. 'All of them starkers rolling about on the beds. Disgusting, indecent fornication, that's what it was. I mean three into two don't go, do it, Sir? 'Taint right'. And he glared at the two poor girls, now barely dressed, standing there in the hall. 'But I had 'em out of it, pretty smart, I can tell you. Clap-ridden whores, that's what they are, Sir. We can't have them ruddy Americans spreading V.D. all over the Med. and taking it back home with them too'.

It was the first time I had heard that the aircrew were American. They didn't often use our Staging Posts and of course we had no disciplinary control over them. Such behaviour might be okay in their own quarters, but we couldn't have it here. I told them so this morning.

In a way I was sorry for the girls, probably not paid, plying their trade, outcasts as usual. But I told the Sergeant to send them packing, which he did, with over-righteous relish. They were quite unabashed and put their tongues out at him!

Really, the things I get into!

Sicilian Scene

Last night Tano, the nice Sicilian doctor, and his wife, Lina, invited me to supper at a friend's house on the sea some miles out of town. It was a pleasant unpretentious place, done with much care and taste, very good food and wine and a very relaxed, happy atmosphere. After supper we just sat on the terrace in the moonlight and chatted. Dozens of fishing boats with their big lamps (to attract the fish) were strung out, like a line of street lamps, over the still water about a mile offshore. Just enough light to see people's faces.

Then friends drifted in, a girl brought her accordion and soon the songs began. Bits of operas, dance tunes and then their own Sicilian songs, which they all knew and sang together. Below the terrace was a path down through the lava rocks to the sea. The moon made an artery of silver across the water. To one side a promontory with the ruins of a castle. Perfect! How can you expect Italians to be anything but sentimental and romantic in such an atmosphere!

No serious conversation, nothing but the most superficial contact, an arabesque of lightheartedness, which goes very well with the language, warm, naive, affectionate, jealous, which here, in this volcanic earth, runs to violence and passion. The vindictive blood feuds, vendettas, come from Sicily. The 'Mafia' stamped on by Mussolini, is already coming back. Al Capone is a Sicilian. So is Sinatra! The contrast, gangster and crooner, somehow symbolize the national character.

The local morals seem extremely strict. No young girl would dream of going out alone with a man. The chance of making a 'respectable' marriage would then be nil! But the marrying age is very young. Fifteen or sixteen is usual. Temptations are understood. After marriage, the rules are just as strict. Many are not allowed out alone at all. Some get as far as doing a little shopping in the mornings. The Sicilian is the epitome of the jealous husband. What he allows himself is another matter.

Back of it all is, of course, the very real power of the Church. Sicily is as badly priest-ridden as Ireland. The fear of hell and damnation is real. To live in a state of Grace, via Confession, Penitence, Absolution and Communion — that most wonderful system of holding society in leading strings — is a convention that all — or almost all — subscribe to. The Italian is, on the whole, deeply religious. I suppose Italy is the most 'moral' country in Europe today. Lina, for instance, the doctor's wife, spends at least an hour every day in her Church! But war, alas, spreads licence. How much of this will last the next decade?

Compassionate Leave

I am sad tonight. We have a Corporal Fitter here, one of the mechanics who looks after the motor vehicles. A quiet unassuming little man, the sort you might find at any country garage, not the top man, just the chap who does the job and keeps you going to the place because you know you can trust his work.

He came to me about three weeks ago with a letter from his wife. It was a scrawly illiterate letter, but it said she was very ill and in great pain and they said she ought to have an operation. She dreaded it and wanted him near her . . . So would I send him home?

It's pathetic the way they think the Commanding Officer can do anything, when he is just as powerless and impotent as they are in things like this. I had to tell him that I couldn't and that the only thing to do was to sit down and concoct one of these 'mental distress' wires. They can only be sent to 'next of kin', they can't be sent to the doctor, but we hoped she would show it to him and he would try to get something done his end. We worded the wire together and sent it off. The days went by and there was no answer. I saw him the other day and stopped to ask him if he had heard anything. He said no, but I was told he had packed his kit and was quite certain he would get away. Today we had a signal saying his wife was dead.

Poor Charlie, my Adjutant, had to break it to him. He was quite stunned. For a while he didn't say anything. Then he managed to get out 'There's nothing left, sir . . .' And burst into tears. Poor little chap. He's never any trouble. You can trust him absolutely. I don't suppose he's cried since he was a kid. He never fusses or grumbles, he just gets on with it. He's England really, the wonderful patient backbone of England that carries the burden of the day and gets nothing out of it. We put him in my office and left him alone with his grief.

Oh, I know a thousand things may have happened. Perhaps she thought she'd be all right and didn't want to worry him. Perhaps it was a slight operation that had turned bad. (Actually it was cancer, but she was probably never told). But the regulations make it pretty well impossible for a man to get home. It has to be certified that his presence will save his wife's life. Who can possibly judge a thing like that? And when it gets serious, how can he possibly get home soon enough?

Of course I understand that the regulations must be strict or everybody would be going home. You can't get back for infidelity, you can't get home for death, you can — in certain circumstances — get home for money. You would, of course, be able to get back for that! — the least important thing out here. But the difficulties are pretty well insurmountable. So what can we do for the poor chap? He's been out here three years. I don't know but it will be all I can . . . (Actually I signalled Whitney personally and, as usual, he came to the rescue. The lad was home within forty-eight hours).

Adjutant and I were talking of the tragedy of these things and he told me of another somewhat similar case he had had to deal with. He had to send for the man and told him, to begin with, that his wife was dangerously ill. 'Oh no, she's not, Sir,' he answered, 'I had a letter from her yesterday. She's fine'. He was jolly and perky, a spunky little chap who'd been out here about two and a half years. His wife had died in childbirth by another man.

I know these are black things and there are plenty who get through all right . . . but it's the feeling that we're all part of a vast implacable machine that grinds and grinds and is quite indifferent to the life of the individual. I suppose it can't be helped. It's just part of the set-up.

But my feeling gets stronger and stronger that the set-up is all wrong. H. G. Wells is right when he says there is a limit to the human being's ability to co-operate. The thing has grown too big for us. The reduction of the individual to a cypher, a number — we refer to men as 'bodies' out here — is strangling the individual and producing the disintegration of society. It's going on all the time and we don't see it. People hate the machine and all it stands for, but they've grown to depend on and can't do without it. We're making our own prison and all the time screaming for liberty! And there are far too many of us! I feel deeply that we've gone wrong. To be reduced to being nonentities can't be the destiny of the human race!

Night Visitor

Just as I sat down to write to you last night the phone rang with a message from the Tower that Ivor was about to land! It was quite unexpected. He had simply called up on the RT about fifty miles away and asked them to warn me. I couldn't get up to the field in time so I arranged for a bed and a meal for him and sat down to wait. I had no idea he was in this part of the world.

He didn't actually land till ten at night — the first night landing he had made for over a year! I wasn't there, but my boys told me that the man he was with, an Australian Sergeant, known as the Baron, landed first and made a nice touchdown while Ivor was still circling above. Ivor enquired how he had made out. 'Fine!' said the Baron 'I'm down okay'. Ivor was then heard to remark, more or less to himself 'I wish to God I was!' However, he made it quite nicely and all was well.

The boy is on Ops now and I think it has done him good. He has much more assurance and poise and when he arrived last night with his parachute over his shoulder and his kit dangling, I felt quite proud of him.

We had a meal and gossiped till midnight. Apparently his Squadron's targets are barges and gunboats along the Yugoslav coast. That means a hundred miles over the sea at low level before getting to the target, then the attack at mast height, then back home again. It's nervy work. Apart from the actual attack, nobody flies over a hundred miles of sea at low level for fun. You may easily have been hit by flak and have engine failure on the way home. I asked him if the flak was heavy. 'Pretty thick,' he said, 'but d'you know, Dad, I don't seem to see it when I'm going in'. He evidently adores his Commanding Officer and is happy in his Mess. His morale is right on the top line which is just as it should be!

This morning he was on his way again. I got out my Hurry and we put the Baron in the lead and formated on him. We gathered some angels* and tucked in tight formation as we sped away over the blue sea. It was a gorgeous morning, waves whitecapped, a few white snow gashes on Etna's black flanks, mist rising over the lowlands and all beyond it Italy! When we reached the Straits — the Scylla and Charybdis of old — I said farewell to them on the RT, swept in a great curve away in the sparking light with the wind at my back, down to the island and the earth again.

*1 angel = 1000 feet

Staging Post Ball

I suppose you wonder how we dare think of arranging a Ball when things are so difficult and serious at home. I do feel a bit guilty about it, but you have to remember that the war has passed us by. There is no action here. Things are very slack and one of our greatest problems is how to keep up morale, how to keep the whole unit, officers and men from getting too discontented and bloodyminded. Entertainments go a long way towards this. We've had concert parties for the men, which did wonders for them. So I thought it was about time the Staging Post officers had something to raise the local morale. Nothing like a good party for that!

Although it was warm and there was a full moon, I decided not to set the thing up out of doors. We had found a disused hall outside the town on the shore. It was a bare barracks of a place, but it had quite a good floor, doors opening on to trees and the sea where we could have places to sit out and I thought if we tarted it up a bit, it would do.

There was a platform for the band at one end and three arches masking the windows at the other. All we had to do was 'dress' it. We went round the town and hired dozens of flowering trees and ferns, oleanders and palms and other prickly and privetty sort of things. We put these all round the room to hide the dirty plaster walls. We sent parties out to cut lashings of pink oleanders, which are now in spate all over the airfield, and put these in old five gallon drums brightly painted. White madonna lilies, roses and carnations we set in milk bottles all round the room. Somehow we got hold of miles of pale blue and pink tissue paper and draped this all round and over the terrible plain hanging lights in the ceilings. The buffet tables were put between the arches with the windows beyond, overlooking the sea. When night came the whole place was transformed. It looked like a bower.

Not having entertained for months the Mess Fund was full! If it gets too full, the Authorities pinch it! So there was no object in not being lavish! We gave our magnificent Sergeant Cook a free hand with the funds. Being in the catering business in civil life he really let himself go and put on such a supper as I have certainly not seen since war began! I won't make your mouth water by giving you the menu, but, well, Sicily makes the best cakes I have ever eaten and is famous for its ices. Palermo is legendary for lobsters and prawns and octopus, while oranges, tangerines, grapes, lemons, olives are products of the country. Add all this up and you can see we had quite a spread!

Our band was an RAF combination which, after oiling, gave full power. By some fluke — and careful selection — we assembled a company of really lovely women. To set off our drab khaki drill, we suggested the girls should wear evening dress. Since they hadn't done that all through the war years, the idea was accepted with alacrity. We also barred all chaperones — the feature of parties out here — where these old crayfish come just to gorge the food! So the invitations read 'No top cover' giving it an RAF turn! We brought this off so well only one chaperone got by — and not by invitation!

The result was really enchanting. We were about eighty strong, pretty well balanced and there was plenty of room on the floor. The profusion of flowers, the soft lights and the long dresses of the women made quite a picture. Outside the Moon shone on the sea. There were Countesses and Baronesses — we didn't run to a Duchess — although there is said to be a local brew and my officers, who had worked like mad on various parts of the thing, managed to produce a batch of lovelies who had my eyes out on stalks! (Some of the enterprising had even provided silk underwear for the occasion!). Of course we'd invited the Army in strength. Both the District and Army Commanders were with us. I wouldn't allow any spirits to be served, but there was plenty of white wine and vermouth so we were all perfectly cheerful.

There was a moment when the party had really got going, about thirty couples were in action on the floor and the band was playing 'Any old night is a wonderful night if you're there with a wonderful girl'. Adjutant and I were standing near the buffet and, looking at it all. I said: 'Quite something to have brought it off, isn't it?' He nodded. 'People will never forget it — just like peacetime'. The vista of hope and longing that one word brought up touched us both. It's all pretty drab and tatty out here and only something like this makes it possible to carry on.

All this was last night and this evening I am dead with fatigue. Such things are really not much fun for the organizers, but looking back on it I think I have rarely been at any party anywhere at any time, which I have enjoyed more. The whole day the phone has been going with congratulations and enquiries as to the next one! But I am too old a hand to get into that. This was a 'One-off!'! And Transport Command is at the top! Where it should be!

Next week I'm going to take a week's leave. I really need it. I've managed to scrounge a small tender (with driver) to make a tour, ostensibly to see the other airstrips on the island! So I'm going to do the famous 'Giro Classico', the round tour of the sights of Sicily. As it's only May I don't think it will be too hot. It's said to be impossible after 15 June. I'm taking a campbed so I can sleep out! I'm rather looking forward to it! (Expect an interval before you get letters.)

I'm two thousand feet up in this little mountain town. There's a gorgeous white wine here, twenty years old they say, heavy and dark, and well, you know how it is with a good wine... I'm on leave! How I wish you were here!

We came south across the Catanian plain and, deciding to miss Syracuse, since I'd seen it before, turned west and ran all afternoon through parched yellow lowlands with their corn-fields rustling ripe and ready for reaping. Then came a big thunderhead as we breasted the first foothills, torrents and torrents of cool rain, splashing and splashing our arms and faces. And then! The loveliest smell in the world — dry countryside after a shower! At last, after long wandering through upsloping country with the promise of mountains before us, we came to this little town, perched on the summits of three hills.

Now as I write in a room on the top floor of an Inn, looking down over a tumbled maze of roofs and gulleys, with the swelling plains and the blue sea far below, the place seems all churches and towers and anvils and blacksmiths and the ringing of hammers and gusts of forges and the twittering of swifts and swallows and choirs of bells . . .

Before dark I climbed the broad stairway to the Citadel, 142 steps, so they say, the whole flanked both sides with tumbledown medieval houses, littered with rubbish and overrun with dozens of squalling children! My how they breed here! It is all part of a feeling I've had before, the whole island is simply bursting with life, fecund like the tropics. When I got to the top the church wasn't worth seeing, but the view was immense, so I sat down near a blacksmith's forge and smelt the sizzling burnt smell of horses' hooves — he was shoeing a mare — and then came slowly down again.

The children accost you all the time, begging for chocolates or cigarettes. The Americans came through here during the invasion and all the children have picked up two phrases, and two only: Okay Joe and F- off! As you can imagine the words came somewhat strangely from the lips of tiny children and when one particularly lovely child invited me to F- off! it set me thinking . . .

I imagined that her parents died and she was brought up by the Nuns. At seventeen she is fully developed and exquisite, peach skin, huge dark eyes, breasts like pomegranates in the season of pomegranates, slim, well turned legs — the way they grow here, in fact perfect beauty in adolescence.

She is walking one summer evening in the piazza with her girlfriend when she is accosted by a young man, whom she has no difficulty in recognizing by his shy reserved manner as an Englishman. Actually he is a young cleric, interested in mediaeval Sicily, Norman remains, etc. etc. and has come to Caltagirone to see the majolica and faience in the churches, for which the place is famous. However he is still young enough to be carried away by the warmth of the evening — and the ravishing beauty of the girl and follows her. When at last he plucks up courage to speak, he tells her of his calling and his interests and asks if he may walk with her. Of course she doesn't speak a word of English but she scents possibilities and recalls one of those dim phrases she had learned in childhood. 'Okay, Joe' she says.

Delighted to find his suit accepted, particularly as his parents had christened him Joseph, and imagining she speaks English, he chatters on, praising the beauty of the country, this little town and, growing bolder, the ravishing beauty of his companion which raises his soul to things for which there are no words, etc, etc. Of course she understands not a single word of this, but the young man is evidently making advances. What can she say to charm and encourage him? She fumbles back in her memory for the only other phrase in English she remembers and smiling deliciously, eyes glowing with gaiety and tenderness, 'F- off!' she says. The young man turns pale, horrified, and rushes back to the arms of his family . . .

The Granary Of Rome

We left Caltagirone early next morning and coasted away down curling white roads through limestone country with wide spreading views like Spain or Algeria. Everywhere miles and miles of grain, ripe, swaying in the breeze. Each swing of the road brought a new and richer vista. At first it was all dominated by Etna, her skirts flounced with olives, almonds and figs, then lower, oranges and vineyards, the valleys bedded with grain and everywhere embroidered with wildflowers, clumps of agave fuming with bees, tall thistles, sprawling wild sweet peas, blue convolvulus, marigolds and a hundred others I have no name for. It is enchanted country.

Then came a sudden temporale*, eclipsing the heat and giving us, in the heart of the downpour, a marvellous silhouette — a tiny donkey, bearing a load of hay twice as big as itself, on top of which sat a child shielding herself with a monstrous big black umbrella, the whole top-heavy vision balanced on four matchstick legs.

But soon the sun was out again and the heat grew. All along the roads were trails of donkeys and mules bearing immense loads of grain. All this country is supposed to have been liber-

*A storm.

ated by Mussolini from extortionate Mafia landlords by giving every peasant family its own home with its own plot of earth.

Whether it has worked or not, that day as we passed they called to us and smiled and seemed happy enough, but we heard the old patterns were coming back. Change is not that easy.

Suddenly round a bend of the road we were confronted by a pyramid! It was so perfect in shape that at first I could not believe that Nature had created such a work of symmetry. It went by the magical name of *La Floresta* and stood about three hundred feet high, closing a vista of sundrenched hills, crowned by summit towns, Mazzarino, San Michele, Campo Bello, all built of this friable yellow limestone. All day we did not see a single mechanical farm implement. Not a reaper or thresher or binder or tractor. Their present was our past — and it was a privilege to see it living.

Later the country grew waterless. The roads were long and dusty. There were green lizards as big as cats and green birds as big as hens. The road surface was atrocious and we clattered across miles of Cezanne country till we reached a death valley of sulphur. But the mines are deserted. They only yielded 18% while the American mines yield 80%.

At last we were glad enough to sight Agrigento and to park the car, white with dust and wash and get a drink in the cool of an hotel. It had been very hot on the road.

Agrigento

I had an introduction to an officer stationed in the little town. His name was Captain Oliver and he turned out to be extremely hospitable and charming. He at once insisted that we should stay with him and his detachment. His quarters were an old 16th century palazzo with a great arched doorway, a dim staircase, majolica tiled floors and a superb ceiling. We rested and sunbathed on his terrace till tea, chatting of this and that. Then he suggested we went to have a look at the famous Temples.

The old Greek settlement was set well below the present town on a sort of shelf between it and the sea. Here the Temples are situated. Below it the ground falls away vertically to the coastal plain now about a mile wide where a new harbour, Porto Empedocle, has been opened up. The sea has long ago receded from the old sea wall below the town.

The Temples are difficult to see at first, their stone matches the earth so closely, but once you have seen them, you begin to get some idea of the way the old city must have lain along this bluff with the sea below. They say that the site has possibilities of excavation equal to Pompeii, but so far it has all been done by an Englishman, Hardcastle, out of his own private fortune. He has confined himself to the Temples, all of which lie along the edge of the plateau.

Originally, it is said, the temples were all faced with stucco, dead white and ornamented in primary colours, reds, yellows and blues, on cornices and friezes. I have a sneaking feeling that they may look more impressive now than they did then! Colour often masks line. I remember seeing the marble head of a woman I once knew. Her colour and vivacity obscured the fact that she had beautiful features. Not until I saw them in marble did I realize it. Are we worshipping as the highest art something which is only its skeleton? How should we feel if Praxiteles turned up with his paints and offered to 'finish' some of his marbles?

As you approach, the first thing that ... es the eye is the Temple of Concord. It is the most perfectly preserved of them all — the most perfect in Sicily. You come upon it from below so that its fluted pillars, its architrave and pediments stand against the sky. The proportions are exquisite, it seems to breathe the harmony its name implies. As you walk the aisles of pillars, seeing the framed views of the perfect countryside, you are transported in a strange way out of the chaos and carnage of today back to the felicity of the Golden Age, an age of pastoral simplicity which sets one longing for a world simple enough for us to cope with and with some values worth living for.

When we had slowly wandered round Concord we walked on to the Temple of Juno. It stands at the end of the bluff, looking down over the river and the sea. Though not so perfect as Concord, Juno is larger and for some reason I cannot explain, seems even more perfect. We just sat on a rock dangling our feet over the two-hundred-foot drop and looked back along the old sea wall. Towering above us were the headless pillars of Juno, then came snug little Concord, then the ruined Hercules and Jupiter (where the huge male statues that once upheld the roof lie prone in the grass) and last of all, far away, hidden in the olives, those four perfect columns of Castor and Pollux — the ones that feature in all the tourist advertisements.

The heat had gone out of the sun. The breeze came off the sea. The place was utterly deserted and still. I could hear goat bells in the olives. Right above was the skyline of Agrigento. 'I come here when I'm, lonely or depressed,' said my friend. I could understand it. Our conversation died away and I actually went to sleep there, sitting in the sun.

The Virgin

As we were changing for supper, I remarked to Oliver on the fine appearance of his maidservant, a great dark Juno of a girl.

'Ah,' he said, 'There's a story for you!'

It appears just prior to our airborne invasion of the island, the girl, born and bred in Agrigento, eloped with an Italian soldier. She was picked up, destitute, on the dockside at Catania, about to do away with herself. A British Officers' Mess took her in as a servant: but she was a bit rough, untrained, singing about the place, so, when Oliver was sent to Agrigento, they suggested that he should take the girl back with him to her home town.

We had a talk with the girl. Her story was that the soldier with whom she had eloped had disappeared, taking with him all the dowry and money she had filched from her parents prior to her flight.

Moreover, she swore that he had never touched her and that she was a 'good girl'. This seemed highly unlikely, given the circumstances and the standards of Sicilian morals.

When Oliver agreed to take the girl he insisted that, as he had a number of men in his charge, and, as the VD rate was very high, she should be examined. The Sicilian doctor called in pronounced her 'virgo intacta!'

'There!' said Oliver 'Can you believe that? In Sicily, of all places!'

I said I flatly refused to believe it. The doctor, I said, knowing that such a certificate was worth its weight in gold, knowing the girl could never go home without it, had exacted 'one heavenly night' as the price of the document.

'In which case,' said Oliver, 'we may well soon have an immaculate conception in Agrigento.'

'And the girl', I added, 'will end up by being canonized as the local Saint!'

So you see we were in very good spirits.

A Strange Shrine

Next morning I climbed to the summit of the town where the Cathedral overlooks both sides of its ridge. It is not an outstanding building, but curious inside because one-third of it is Norman of the 11th century, one-third probably Spanish of the 13th and the remainder rococo of the 18th. The Norman part had a wonderful old wooden roof and in one of the small chapels a Greek sarcophagus in white marble, wonderfully serene and restful.

I wandered down the town through narrow smelly streets, often changing to steps they are so steep and went into the Monastery of St Spirito. The old courtyard, well and garden were very dignified and quiet, but the little church was one of the most fantastic I have ever seen. Imagine a small room entirely overlaid, walls and ceiling, with every sort of angel, madonna or saint, with urns and shields and swords and banners, a crucifixion scene, a nativity scene and others I did not recognize, all, but ALL, moulded in high relief out of DEAD WHITE PLASTER OF PARIS!

It was like some monstrous religious wedding cake gone mad. The fat old Mother Superior who showed me round was obviously frightfully proud of it and hardly deigned to show me the rest of the place!

By now it was very hot and I made my way down to the palazzo. On one bit with twisting flights of steps on either side, women were threshing their pittance of corn. Girls or old women were crouching low, beating the grain with a light flail. It was such a contrast between wealth and poverty. While the place is overrunning with fertility, there were these people, miserably poor, sweating over a miserable heap of grain on a white sheet in a doorway!

Terra Ballerina

The road from Agrigento drops down to the new port, Porto Empedocle. We stopped here for a moment to watch the sardine fleet coming in to anchor. Red, yellow and blue sails on a very blue sea under a burning sky.

Then the road wound along through barren limestone hills and turned inland towards Menfi. This stretch was very fine, broad valleys casting away and away to high mountains dappled with cloud shadows, all, when you looked closer, capped with hill towns. One range was so straight and curling it looked like a breaking wave of stone.

Through this some attempt had been made to beautify the roads. For miles we drove through hedges of red geraniums! Then hedges of pink and white oleanders! Georgeous, but it seemed somehow too sophisticated for the country which remained lonely and desolate in the glare of too much sun and sea.

At last we turned off the main road and drove down to the coast to see our next set of ruins. These were at a place called Selinunte. They stand on either side of a sandy hollow that was once a harbour. There are two Temples on the East and three on the West side of it and the whole lot have been rattled absolutely flat by an earthquake which, at the same time, lifted the whole harbour thirty feet above sea level! This somewhat interferred with its value as a port and the place has remained a sort of abomination of desolation ever since.

This part of the world the Italians call 'terra ballerina' — a charming phrase. Certainly this 'waltzing earth' has a sort of exciting gaiety about it that justifies the name. In the fresh breezes of this time of the year, the glare of the sun and the profusion of flowers and crops seem to set the whole landscape dancing, whirling in a sort of ecstacy; but here, in a second, the dance must have turned to the horrors of death, for we were looking at, literally, acres of fallen columns - great drums of honey-coloured stone — lying about in the most disordered abandon.

You can still see the old harbour walls, the quays, the remains of streets and one magnificent line of columns, still erect and standing, having somehow withstood the violence of the disaster. We clambered about this graveyard of destruction and I picked up a tiny clay head and a small pot among the rubble. In a house overlooking the shore is a sort of Museum, where some of the better remains are housed. There was also a reconstruction drawing of the whole place as it had been when it was a 'going concern' — a striking contrast to what was outside the window! Now there is no human habitation for miles, just a flat coast, a windy sea and ruin. We didn't stay long and left the sad old custodian anxiously enquiring if Rome had fallen — ten days after the event!*

* General Mark Clark entered Rome on 4 June, 1944.

Had you ever heard of the Egadi Islands off the West Coast of Sicily? I certainly hadn't. I vaguely knew there was tunny fishing somewhere off the coast and now I was in the area, I thought it would be interesting to see it. I was told it took place on the island of Favignana. So I went to Trapani, a sleepy, dusty little town on the coast opposite the island, to find a ferry to take me over.

On the quay I was lucky enough to meet a native of Favignana, speaking fluent American! It turned out he had come home to see his family and had been caught there by the War. He was very friendly and hospitable and offered to put me up. There was no taverna on the island, he said.

As the ferry chugged its way out of port, we could see the demolition the Italians had carried out before our arrival. Very half-hearted! Just bits of the quays blown into the water, a hole in the mole. Nothing to stop the place getting working again in a couple of days. The fact that there is practically no tide in the Med means there is no need to build up the quays. This gives their ports a brimming-over effect, as if it was always high tide. It makes the shore line very attractive and picturesque.

As we cleared the harbour we could see Favignana about eight miles away, a mountainous island with two Norman castles, no roads, a little port and the tunny factory. Half-way between Trapani and Favignana is a tiny island, called La Formica (the ant). This is nothing but a lighthouse and fishing sheds. Off both these islands are the nets. As we chugged along my new friend told me how the fishing is done.

Nobody knows how many centuries ago some fishermen discovered that at certain seasons of the year, the tuna 'run' along this coast and found out the way to net them. They laid out a 'wall', or guide net, over a mile long and about 50 feet deep, just hanging down from floats on the surface. Of course the tuna, famous for their deep sounding when taken on the line, could easily swim beneath the net. But they don't. Reason —

and goofy, all thousand pounds of them, following the girl friend about, just waiting for her to spawn, so they can impregnate her eggs. So they amble along the length of the nets just staying about 30 feet below the surface (nobody knows why) and run straight into the traps.

These traps are called 'rooms'. There are three of them. Each is about the size of two tennis courts and all are quite open at the bottom, but their 'cross' walls, at either end, can be opened or closed, like doors. The placid unsuspecting fish, dazed by their love impulse, do not notice the first cross wall being closed behind them. All is clear ahead. But as they go further, another cross wall closes behind them and the first is opened to admit more fish. So, at the season when the 'run' is on, day by day the number of fish increases, all swimming idly into the traps, room by room, still hypnotized by their sexual urges, and at last all find themselves in a fourth room.

But this room (called *La camera di morte!*), unlike the others, has a bottom. A strong closely meshed wire net, lying loosely, joining the side walls and fastened to booms floating on the surface. For days the fishermen have been watching the tuna arriving through small glass-bottomed boats and counting up the number of fish they have trapped in the last 'room'. When it reaches an agreed number, about 200, a notice is displayed on a blackboard, on the island of Formica, large enough to be seen on the mainland at Trapani, five miles away.

This brings other fishermen out with their heavy boats and barges. All of them tie up to the booms that surround the trap. When the Priest has blessed the catch, the word is given and over a hundred men all lining the booms start to raise the nets, pulling them up hand over hand.

Then begin those terrible pictures of carnage you may have seen on the movies. The big fish, fighting to escape, boil the sea into a white cauldron of foam and fury, while the fishermen impale them with long spears and throw them over their shoulders into the boats behind. When the 'bottom' is high enough, some men leap into the water, wading on the nets in the raging

66

foam and blood to impale the biggest fish to kill them before they can be hoisted over the booms to the boats. The huge fish, so beautiful, their shining silver armour, flailing their neighbours in their mad death agonies, make an unforgettable picture of horror at what hunting can become when wild Nature is cornered to be massacred by man.

I am glad I did not have to see it, for there were only a few fish in the 'rooms', not enough to justify a 'catch'. Instead I was shown over the factory, very tidy and clean, but with a nauseating stink of fish over everything that almost made me sick! After boiling, dozens of big fish were hanging up on hooks, prior to being filleted into all sorts of different 'cuts' for despatch, I suppose, all over the world. Nothing is wasted. Even the bones are ground down to make cattle food and manure. I was presented with a small piece of tuna liver! I tried it for supper. Ugh! It was rich.

Supper was, of course, the usual family affair with all the generations present. It consisted entirely of different sorts of tunny and finished after midnight! It was endlessly hospitable, friendly and affectionate, but too much for me. I was ashamed of myself for feeling such a loner and being so glad to get away. But I don't think they noticed it.

Communism

This morning, having slept in an empty house nearby, I came back from Favignana. The morning was something to uplift the heart! Blue, sunflecked sea, mauve mountains and at their feet the little white port of Trapani. Nearby windmills turning at the saltpans. Behind the town the isolated crag of Erice, towering three thousand feet and capped with a citadel which dates back to the Greeks.

I chatted with some of the other passengers on the way over. The country is seething with anger about the black market. The price of bread and all commodities is fantastic. Flour is being kept out of the shops by rings and combines lining their pockets at the expense of the peasants. I noticed many communist signs. The hammer and sickle is everywhere stencilled on the walls. The men I talked with seemed to have little sympathy with the ideas, but they said that the communists at least had a policy which nobody else had!

Meanwhile beautiful rich little Sicily, which need want for nothing, is near starvation! It doesn't seem much of a start to the brave new world we have been shouting about for the last four years! Sicily is our first foothold in Europe and it ought to be the shopwindow for the benefits of democracy. Instead our rank and file have less dignity and discipline than the enemy. It is the old story. No rules of conduct because there are no standards, no standards because there is no belief. It always comes back to that.

Erice

In the afternoon we drove up the lonely crag of Erice. The road, like an alpine pass, twists this way and that in S-bends, climbing round the flanks to the peak, giving tremendous views of the curving coast and the country below, laid out like a map. Often the road ran so precariously you could see nothing but sky from the seat of the car, just like being airborne! The little white port of Trapani below owes its name to the sickle bay on which it stands and goes back to the old days. Trepan, I believe, is the Greek word for sickle. As we climbed higher we could see southward down the coast to Marsala (now more than the name on a bottle!) and north to Cap San Vito. Of all the marvellous views in Sicily, I think this is the most impressive.

Erice, the little village which caps the crag, seems almost like a Cornish hamlet, whitewashed, cobbled and quiet in the cool upper air. The streets are narrow. Through doorways are courtyards with ferns and flowers. The clouds drift by like mist. At the summit are some diminutive public gardens with a toy bandstand. Nearby stands the castle. Like Troy the place is really an archaeological sandwich. Greek, Roman, Saracen, Norman, Frank, Spaniard — all have coveted this impregnable eyrie and have used it while their power lasted, all have left their mark on walls and battlements, towers and dungeons. Curiously, after all this it seems awfully English! The same misty air, the same grey-lichened walls, over-run with ivy and tiny ferns, the same sleepy peace. There were bits of tessellated Roman pavements, rough Norman arches and hearths. Part of one of the towers had been made into a private residence! From one turret I could see half Sicily! On lower spurs were Saracen churches and a Spanish barracks, both whitewashed. Round the whole place a pine forest has been planted which scents the air. It was really all quite magical. Unique.

We wandered about for a bit and then came down on another road so steep and twisty we had to reverse on some of the corners!

Segesta

I am sitting in a little dungeon-like room in Palermo — exhausted! It seems a week since we left Trapani. And it was only this morning! We really have been cramming too much into too short a time and I am so full of impressions that all these letters must sound like a tourist guide! I had no idea that Sicily would overwhelm me as it has.

We left Trapani early so as to run cool for a bit — it is really too hot here after June 15 — and made for Segesta, the last of the famous ruins on the island. It wasn't till we got near the place, up among wild peaks and steep-sided valleys that we realized how secret, how aloof it was.

It really is a mystery place. Temples naturally imply people, and people a town. At Segesta, though there is a temple, and a theatre, there is no town, no village, no remains, as far as anyone can find, of any settlement of any kind!* Excavations have been made, archaeologists have combed the adjacent hills and valleys, but nothing more than a few coins have ever been unearthed.

And, on top of all that, the place is unfinished! How did it come to be built? Was it some garden city project abandoned before it was finished? Nobody knows. Meanwhile at intervals along the curling road, alone among the mountains, you get glimpses of this grey shell of pillars, this elfin hall of ghosts, serene and somehow wistful, lost and forgotten except by the few who find time to make the pilgrimage.

How to give you a picture of the place? It is all feeling, all atmosphere. First it is confined, hidden in mountains dark in tone, blues, greys and blacks, amid smooth upslopes of heath and dry grass. One has a feeling of shadowy loneliness, 'of flutes and oboes, of calling echoing tunes that only Delius could have written. More nostalgic, more poignant perhaps this morning because of the great wind that filled the air with wings.

We walked up the slope and saw it there above us! Lord, it was beautiful! Just a shell of pale honey-coloured stone, standing on columns, cornice, frieze and architrave, up, up, goes the eye and only checks at the wild flowers tufting out from cracks and crannies that crown the stone.

The Temple floor is a meadow. Between the columns are clouds one never sees in the north. One sweeps like a great wing across the sky, others are so queerly ribbed and shaped, they seem like the background to some primitive painting which those who have never seen them would think just invented formalities. All this seemed to heighten the simplicity. No man-made place I ever saw seemed so remote, the world forgetting by the world forgot. We just sat on the plinth in the great wind, felt the sun scorching our arms and faces and gazed over the view those builders must have seen when they first raised this place of wonder more than two thousand years ago!

* Lots have since been found.

Palermo

Whether it was the wonderful start or just the way the road went I don't know, but it seemed the whole day was enchanted. What country! Crescents of blue sea, turquoise-lipped, eating into green bays, at either horn a mountain for a sentinel! The earth simply teeming with crops, the ripe corn like a sea of gold lapping against orchards of orange and lemon and regimented vines! I often think the test of a place is: Should we like to live here? The answer is definitely YES! Of all our days, today was the loveliest and that's saying something after all these letters!

We came to a village called Partinacci. The road was rising now towards the barrier of mountain that backs Palermo. We had reached the extreme north-western tip of the island and had only the pass ahead before reaching the capital. We climbed on and up to a mountain village called Montelepre where a clock had been set in a Norman tower far too big for this little place, hanging by its eyelids to the mountain side.

Now it was like the approach to the Gothard or the St Bernard, windy empty mountains, lakes and falls of scree. We must have been over 4000 feet and it was blessed cool. We came to the saddle of the Pass and suddenly — there was the sea!

From the road the earth dropped in a steep parabola down to the orange groves and villages below. A little islet, La Femina, stood in the bay. The mountains rose on both sides. This sudden view was breathtaking. Then, after more hairpins, we swung right — and stopped! Below lay Palermo!

I suppose no small capital in the world has such a magnificent setting. The white city is set like a pearl on the seashore, backed by its famous *concho d'oro*, the golden shell of its orange groves. On all three sides the mountains hold it close. The Sacramento — with shrine to the Patron Saint of Sicily, Santa Rosalie — juts up on one side. Behind, on an eminence, stands Monreale, a Norman church which, except for Istanbul, boasts the most famous mosaics in the world. Perched high above all this on our mountain road, sunlight behind us, we gazed down over it in the golden haze of evening. It was the climax of the whole week and, having exhausted all my superlatives I promise to be prosaic from now on!

Antiques

I was up at 8.15 and spent most of the morning rubber-necking the churches. Most of them seem to cluster fairly closely round the Quatro Canti, the main crossroads of the city. There were fine mosaics in the Palatine Chapel and a perfect Saracen Shrine with domes like pierced pepperpots. I didn't want to overdo it, as I've already seen too much, so I just wandered about. The whole town seemed busy and lively, obviously happy to be out of the War and rid of Mussolini. I was much attracted to a very amusing baroque fountain standing near the Quatro Canti. It must be fun when the water comes out of the beasts in the centre of the main basin. These queer creatures out of the Book of Revelation are a contrast to the alternating male and female figures on the circular rim, all looking away from each other and frowning — not unnaturally, since the artist, with a perverted sense of humour, has carved them grimly hiding their private parts with their hands! All very Italian.

I went to pay my respects to the parents of the Agrigento family who had entertained me so charmingly when I passed through. I found an elderly distinguished couple in a spacious apartment. I had been told the man was a collector, but was quite unprepared for what I saw. There was nothing later than the 17th century. Every piece seemed perfect of its kind. There were beautiful chairs and tables made of 'violet ebony' — whatever that may be — Venetian chandeliers, very ornate, a ridiculous wrought iron fourposter, if you can imagine such a thing, with its lemon damask canopy and gilded crown. There were cases of Sicilian silverwork, earrings and medallions, some early faience tiles and lot of beaten silver work, typically Sicilian, very beautiful, which I had never seen before. It was like fresh air to

72

find all this, cherished and cared for, at a time when everything seems run down.

The old gentleman loved his collection. When everybody was rushing out of Palermo, fearful of the arrival of the Allies, and for some days there was no government and some looting, he stayed put, drove off several parties of thieves and then went out to interpret for the Mayor and the arriving American General. He was evidently glad to meet someone who saw the beauty of his collection, praised my *occhio* and planned a trip we could do together 'after the war'.

Home Run

Then the nightmare started. We have been too slow, in spite of our rush and there was a long run along the north coast of the island to reach a place called Milazzo for the night. I suppose it might have been lovely had I been fresh and not tired from sitting too long in the cramped seat of the tender.

On this road the retreating Hun had blown all the bridges, dozens of them, and at each we had to make the rough detour down to the stream beneath, cross it, struggle up again and soldier on to the next. Very tiring. We only stopped once to visit the great church at Cefalu, where there is a huge mosaic of Christ, backing the altar. But the place was closed, so that will have to be for the next time. At last we turned off the awful road up the isthmus of Milazzo where they grow the earliest tomatoes — and slept, tired out.

The next morning we were off again to Messina. We climbed the narrow gorge and when we reached the summit, paused to look down over the double view. Ahead were the Straits and beyond, so close it seemed impossible, the steep mountains above Reggio and, on the other side of the narrow waters, Italy. It was one last superb prospect, but we had seen all we could and ran down the coastal road, lunched at Taormina and spent the afternoon sunbathing and relaxing on the beach. The first time we had really stopped all week!

Got home to find a concert party had turned up (Leslie Henson, great fun, and girls — very pretty). The whole unit laughed and sang together in the big dining room and, then, (seeing the girls, and all of them starved for sex, poor devils) got drunk. Before the evening was out most of them were very much the worse for wear. I suppose these travelling parties must be used to this sort of thing, but I think some of the girls don't quite know how to handle it.

Anyway, one of them, I suppose for protection, asked if I would see her home. Of course I said I'd be delighted. There were a lot of our chaps in the streets. Some of them, when they saw us, calling and whistling. She said what a wonderful lot of boys I had and how lovely it was to be able to amuse them for an hour or two, then turning her head with a sad smile, 'I know what it is to be lonely too!' We turned into a quiet side street where her rooms were. She was sweet, small and cuddly and when she allowed me to kiss her and touch her . . . well, after about six months celibacy, things tend to catch fire . . .

She asked me, so gently, so tentatively, if I would care to see her up to her room — and writing this to you, the following afternoon — I feel there may have been some feeling of compassion in offering herself, knowing how men are, knowing perhaps from her own life the ache, the loneliness . . . oh, I don't know, but it touched me deeply.

Suddenly all sorts of mixed feelings came up in me. My desires withered. I took her hands, leant down at the door and kissed her like a brother. Partly I think it was because I knew we had been seen and it would be all over the unit the next day. Why should I have the luck, just because I was the CO? But more than that, somehow I felt it wasn't fair — stupid I suppose, but I am proud of my command, jealous of the efficiency and high morale of the unit and I didn't feel it was right for me to have what they couldn't have. I shouldn't feel clean . . . Six months ago I would never have believed I could have such feelings!

P.S. There are rumours of changes, promotions, but I don't want to leave Sicily — except to come home — to you!

Into Greece

Posting

Whitney has been through on one of his lightning whirlwind tours. I like the way he enjoys everything and always make a point of giving him a good lunch! Anyhow he seemed quite pleased with me. I am to leave Sicily. He is giving me the new Staging Post that is being formed to go into Athens when we 'liberate' Greece. I gather it is one of the plum jobs. It means getting my third ring and I suppose I ought to be pleased. But, truthfully, I feel awfully dead about it.

I have been out here nine months — it seems nine years! When I got here last January there was nothing. Just one old shack on the airfield and very low morale. Now there is everything a fully equipped unit ought to have: offices, M.T. Parks, good quarters and food for the men, stores, a laundry and an excellent Officers' Mess in the Hotel and everything running smoothly.

But it has been an uphill job, with little help from the outside, largely the result of my own initiative and effort — and, of course, knowing the language. During these months we have put something like three thousand aircraft through to the front line and given beds and food to thousands of aircrew. I was beginning to enjoy the fruits of my labours. Now I shall have to start the whole thing all over again. Well, I suppose it will be good for me.

Preparations

I have left the island now and moved up into Italy. There is the usual bustle and tension you always get at the beginning of things. This part of Italy is all olives and dust and somehow much poorer than Siciliy, less fruit and vegetables, less colour — and, of course, simply crawling with troops.

It is much cooler too, no mosquitoes, and I am the guest of a Transport Squadron which has a fine mess, so my personal comfort is greater than I had expected.

The Operational RAF Command, under Geoffrey Tuttle, have been more than usually affable and seem prepared to leave everything to me. Somebody must have given me a build up! I have taken a fancy to the SASO, a chap called Bill Foley, almost as tall as I am! He has a nice drawling sense of humour and always seems to be doing nothing, but is actually as sharp as can be. One of the best parts of a job like this is that you always get the pick of the troops. I have some excellent officers and men already and more coming.

Now that I have got through the first depression I am beginning to apply myself with my usual vigour! It helps to get through the days. And there is a job to be done, after all — our first real re-entry into Europe — and we might as well put up a show.

Trulli

Ivor came through on leave. He has passed his commissioning board and will put up his thin blue line soon. He is still on Ops and seems to be doing well. Pity he's turned up now when I'm so busy; but I'll try to take the day off and spend it with him.

I thought we might go and have a look at Trulli — those queer little circular houses I'd seen from the air when I escorted him with the Baron back to his unit some while ago. Now they are quite close to our airfield at Bari. Ever since I saw those little clustering groups of pixie houses, I'd wanted to visit them.

We took my jeep and drove south through the olives. The trees were very old here, their weary trunks held up on columns of stone. It is said you can still stand under an olive as old as the one Christ knelt under in the Garden of Gethsemane.

As we drove south the character of the country changed. It grew cleaner and more cared for. All the houses were freshly whitewashed or painted in pinks and mauves. We turned away from the coast up towards the escarpment inland.

Now the road began to wind through undulating country, mostly vineyards and orchards: but the views were seldom wide, the hills seemed to close in the vistas of the countryside. There were small properties owned by peasant families — and on every hilltop stood a trulli.

Imagine a circular hayrick, its conical roof of grey stone, its walls whitewashed — that is a trulli. Imagine the roof slope slightly concave, like a Chinese roof, and a cup and ball, like an enormous pin's head transfixing the whole place to the ground through its apex. Add white crosses painted on the roof tiles, tiny doll's house windows and little archway doors and cluster three or four of these little places together, and you begin to get some idea of the pixillated enchantment of these diminutive palaces as far removed from the architecture of our days as those pictures of medieval life in *Les Très Riches Heures du Duc du Berry*.

As we drove, coming on more and more of these clusters, our immediate association was with Hansel and Gretel or the drawings of Arthur Rackham. At any moment one could expect the arrival of witches on broomsticks. After passing the village of Locorotondo we felt we wanted to know what sort of people lived in these little places. So we decided to gatecrash the next attractive cluster. This took us down a twisting lane into a tiny courtyard.

We created a sensation! There have been no troops whatever in this corner of Italy and the arrival of the RAF was an event.

They at once invited us to look round and we soon saw that this cluster of trulli was (like most of them) the home of many families. In addition there were many guests, as it was *vendemmia* and the grapes were just about to be pressed. This is an annual festival, a time of great rejoicing. The townsfolk go to their relatives in the country to tread the wine and everyone gets a bit squiffy. We soon made friends with these simple people. There were the usual rabble of children, girls in gipsy colours, elders with crippled legs or wall eyes, but they all had Italian high spirits and started showing us around.

Inside the trulli each room is plastered up to its apex, so you get these little circular rooms about 12 feet across, each with its conical ceiling, immaculately white and clean. Each room leads through an arched doorway to the next and the apparently casual way all the trulli are grouped together is in fact quite well engineered. There is a stairway up the outside of the wall that leads to a broad gutter all round the base of the roofs. All the conical roofs stand on this common gutter, like a table cruet, and when it rains, these gutters are all graded so that the rain from all of them falls into a single barrel below.

I was amazed at their roof tiles too. I thought they'd be like our old west country tiles, but they were actually made of flat stones, two inches thick! They were really walls, each course of stones set slightly back on the one below, the whole making a massive cone! No wonder the walls are thick! It must have been a highly skilled job making them. They are beautifully finished. And, best of all, the trade is not dead. Trulli are still being made today.

The families followed us about everywhere, laughing and joking all the time. In their wine store they proudly showed us their underground cistern, a big plastered cave into which they tipped all the fresh wine. They said it held ten thousand litres. It was covered with a stone lid which they slid back and dropped in a crock tied with a piece of string. It came up running with amber wine and we each drank from it in turn. It was heady and cool and we stood around chatting while they picked us a bas-

79

ket of fresh green almonds we thought we could take back to the Mess.

At last we left with many *auguries* and *buon viaggios* and drove on to another village called Alberobello. This is a National Monument, the whole village, even the Church being trullis. It reminded us of Cornwall. Built on either side of a diminutive valley, the little places seemed to cling together, till I felt you could imagine the whole thing hidden under a mushroom!

As we drove home, we tried to imagine why, in the whole world there should be only one tiny pocket of architecture like this. Where did it originate, what does it derive from? Nobody really seems to know. Of course it is part of the world that has been washed with conquest from time immemorial. Phoenicians, Etruscans, Minoans, Greeks, Persians must all have left colonies and some fragment has survived here. To help its survival Mussolini made a law, reducing taxes on houses built in the trulli manner, but allowed them to have an 'ordinary' ground floor with the little round roofs above. A number have been built. They look quite pretty. The design has come off. Let's hope they build more of them.

We made one last stop, at the most picturesque of all. The little pixillated place stood on a slope. It had only four cones and a ridiculous diminutive cone for a fireplace and chimney. When we knocked and stooped to get through the low door, we found a little old lady in a lavender dress, sitting spinning goat's wool from a pannier and winding it on to a large shiny bobbin. The place was all white, absolutely spotless, you could have eaten off the floor. There were tiny sacred pictures on the walls and willow panniers with tomatoes and peppers standing drying in the deep window ledges.

The little old lady was perfectly at her ease. We giants intruding into her home did not disturb her in the least. We looked around us and said nice things and then made to withdraw; but she would not hear of us leaving till we had met her grand-nieces, whom we could hear whispering in the next room. They turned out to be young girls, of about 14 to 15. They had been to a nearby town to buy buttons and had been resting. They were also quite at their ease with us, and made a point of showing us their room, of which they were very proud. It was chaste as if made for a Nun. Perfectly white. White walls, white coverlets, white curtains and the lovely cone of the ceiling. The whole place gave such an impression of simplicity and purity we left with quite heavy hearts, having glimpsed for a moment a life more perfect than we should ever know.

We drifted back over the edge of the hills away from this secret country and stopped on the coast at a blackmarket restaurant for dinner. An old castle set on a cliff, with no roof but stars and the windowless windows staring down over the sea.

Vendemmia

I oughtn't really to be flying this Hurricane. I've scrounged it because Records seem to have lost it and aren't shouting to have it back to rot in some store. So, until they do I'm getting a lot of fun out of it. I even brought it with me over here and flew it back again a couple of days ago — officially, to get some kit, actually to go up Tre Castagne with the Russos for the vendemmia.

It was a wonderful morning when I took off and I found I could go straight over the top of the mountains of Calabria right in the toe of Italy. At 8000 feet I cleared them easily and coasted down the island to land at Catania. It had taken me an hour and a half. Etna and the island looked so wonderful I found myself quite excited to be coming back.

I phoned the Russos who seemed glad to hear my voice and insisted I stayed with them. We chatted and exchanged news, took a siesta (it's still pretty hot in the island even at the end of September), had a lovely Sicilian supper, freshwater fish, melon and lots of dry wine. Bed at 9.30.

Next morning we all went up to Tre Castagne to see the vendemmia. You remember I told you I was up here earlier in the year when they 'aired' the Saints. Unfortunately when we got there it was so high up that they won't be harvesting the grapes for another fortnight, so we had to be content with just walking round the vineyards.

There is something about this place. When I last saw it in the spring, it was full of promise, full of *allegria* and the grapes were no bigger than pinheads erect on their shoots, but now they are ripe and heavy, huge clusters of clear jade or blue-black marble glowing through the leaves and so profuse you can hardly squeeze your way between the rows. And the rows seem to go on for miles, sweeping away below down the sun-drenched slopes of Etna to the sea. Round the outhouses were little arbours all looped and festooned with garlands of grapes. They had climbed into the fig trees, twined up the iron railings to the terraces. You could feel them ripening in the blessed light, you could feel the goodness of the earth underfoot. It had all that vigorous vibrant fecundity I have spoken of before, life simply bursting out of the earth in joy. Remember Andrew Marvell? . . .

> *What wonderous life is this I lead!*
>   *Ripe apples drop about my head;*
> *The luscious clusters of the vine*
>   *Upon my mouth do crush their wine;*
> *The nectarine and curious peach*
>   *Into my hands themselves do reach;*
> *Stumbling on melons as I pass,*
>   *Insnar'd with flowers, I fall on grass.*

We wandered about for ages, picking bunches of the ripe, warm fruit. Then an old gardener appeared with a platter of ripe figs. We couldn't resist these and then when we had been thoroughly greedy were taken into the *palmetto*.

This is the name given to the barn where the grapes are trodden. It is very old and primitive. Half the barn floor is raised to make three large stone cisterns about twelve feet square. The centre one is higher than the others and it is into this that the grapes are thrown. They are piled up till the tank is full and then young men in shorts with spiked clogs on their feet, jump into it and start dancing on the grapes. They sing as they dance and the crushed juice runs out into the side cisterns and others at ground level. It needs a lot of strength and endurance to keep up the dancing and only the young can do it.

When the grapes are all crushed to pulp they bring in big circular shields of wattles about five feet across. These are placed flat on the pulp and the dancing goes on on top of them. The pips and skins which finally remain are shovelled out into another cistern over which there is an enormous press. This has a whole tree trunk for an arm and a screw a full foot in diameter. I never saw such a screw! This contraption presses a lid down on the last of the pulp. the final residue is put out to dry and crushed later to make crude alcohol.

After the juice has been left to ferment for some days it is pumped through into the next barn. This contains barrels about twelve feet high and sixteen feet long, a whole row of them, each holding about 40,000 litres. When I exclaimed at the size I was assured that this was nothing out of the common — there were plenty much bigger!

No doubt methods of treading the wine differ all over the world. The Sicilian method is very primitive and hasn't changed for centuries. I think what is special is the songs they sing, the festive gaiety of it all. Rosa told me how in her childhood she remembers the scent of the wine hanging about the streets, everyone a little tipsy from the fumes, how the girls that bring in the grapes on their heads sing and dance to encourage the boys in the vats, how they sup together when darkness falls, still reeking from the juice and scent of it all. In the rich districts where the harvest is heavy and there are many vineyards this festive atmosphere may last for weeks till all the grapes are in.

Promotion

I came back this morning. Another perfect run: one hour twenty. I found my third ring had come through! So I have now climbed back to the dizzy height of Wing Commander which I reached in the Air Ministry back in 1940! To commemorate I stood drinks all round. For about fifty chaps, from six till eight, it cost me £8. Imagine what it would have cost me back home!

I do seem to land the tricky jobs. Forming a new Staging Post from scratch presents all sorts of problems; but I'm beginning to find it fun. Starting up a new show makes everybody keen and co-operative and although there are plenty of headaches you don't get that sickening feeling of sagging morale.

Combined Ops

Yesterday I had my first insight into the technique of planning a 'combined operation'. Everyone has marvelled at the organization of the Normandy landings. Few, except those concerned in it, can have any idea of its complication or magnitude. Even for a sideshow like ours the work seems endless.

We all met at HQ to get the general picture from the AOC. It was fascinating. Briefly when an operation involving Army, Navy and Air Force is planned, the first thing is for the Combined Chiefs of Staff to get together and decide what forces are necessary (or can be spared) to carry out the operation. There is a small body of 'crystal gazers' who give an estimate of requirements, a sort of hypothetical stab at what ought to be necessary. These forecasts are, I believe, astonishingly accurate and when the various commands have chewed it over and tossed alternative plans around for weeks or months, they usually come back pretty near to what they started with.

So far it is only a plan to be filed and put aside until the operation is ordered. When it is 'on', the required forces have to be allocated and detailed, together with their equipment, transport, supplies, kit, rations, etc and assembled at the despatching points. All this is a large undertaking in itself requiring a tremendous amount of detailed work. But the headaches do not really start until the question of priorities turns up.

Who must get there first? Who goes in by air and who by sea? How many aircraft or ships are required to porter personnel and supplies? How much can follow up later? In what order should it follow up? Are they available? What supplies are needed at once? Transport is essential, signals are essential, food is essential, arms are essential. But what is most essential? Each unit considers its claims paramount and tries to elbow the others out of the way. Changes of plan occur, sometimes at high level, as a result of later intelligence, or enemy movements or reconsideration of objectives. This means alterations all down the line. A hundred and one queries come up. What will be the state of the tide? This may govern zero hour. How many daylight hours are there? This governs the number of trips transport aircraft can make in the day and thus the loads that can be delivered. There is always the worry of weather. Some things cannot be forseeen. If the beaches are mined the first ships may be blown up. These losses must be replaced. If the wind is high parachute troops may lose men through broken bones on landing. And so on.

I have mentioned a few contingencies out of the hundreds that may arise, but you can see that the chaps responsible for working out the movement and landing schedules go pretty well off their heads as the plan reaches its final stages. Eventually the Movements Officer — the chap who finally carries the can — if not committed to hospital with a nervous breakdown — produces a document setting out every detail of the show. This is the Bible of the Operation and may run to hundreds of pages.

Meanwhile each unit commander has his own problems. Mine are worse than most. I have to consider who will be most important at the other end. Our job will be the unloading of the airborne stuff as it arrives. I must have Traffic Officers and

Clerks to check it and tell officers in charge where to find their stuff at organized dumps. I must have cooks to feed the men and, in the case of aircraft breakdown, fitters and riggers to repair them. But all these men cannot go by air. Some must be there in the first aircraft, some can arrive by sea. (If all goes well they should arrive simultaneously). The sea party will have to bring all the heavy kit, the tents, the stores, the transport. They will have to start earlier so must be sent ahead to the embarking points. They may be delayed by bad weather. Alternatively the Airborne part may also be delayed by bad weather. So we must have men of each trade in both parties.

All this would be fairly easy if I had all my unit with me: but I haven't! Originally the operation was all to start from Egypt, but the way the war has progressed it is now to be mounted partly from Egypt and party from Italy. The result is I have a skeleton party of men and transport and stores with me here and the remainder is back in the Delta. The men have been drawn from units all over the Middle East. I don't know them or the officer in charge of them. Some of the key men are missing from my party and some of the equipment too, and all the paper work — making Nominal Rolls and Daily Routine Orders, etc. (which is being done in an office with five other units trying to do the same thing, sharing one telephone and one ropey type-writer) is extremely difficult. In addition my Adjutant, whose normal business would be to look after all this work, has just been posted to me and turns out to be a Balloon Officer! In civil life he is a builder, and has never held a post like this in all his service career! He's a willing and intelligent chap: but, of course, the whole thing is a mystery to him so far and, though he's putting up a good show, you can imagine time doesn't exactly hang heavy on my hands.

Loading Aircraft

It's been a hectic day again. Our little party won't be enough to unload all the aircraft that will come pouring in on D-Day, so we are going to train some of the RAF Regiment boys, who are coming along in on the first wave, in the mysteries of unloading Dakotas.

We borrowed an aircraft, made up a dummy load and set the parties at it in batches of ten. After a bit of practice they managed to unload three tons in a little under eight minutes. Pretty good going. As the aircraft will have twenty minutes on the ground (we hope) it gives us a nice margin. The AOC came out to see the fun and was quite impressed. My Traffic Officer, Richardson, shoots a very convincing line and, as he really does know his stuff, I feel that this side of the job is one that I really haven't got to worry about. It's a great relief to be able to trust a man and leaves me free to attend to other things.

Greek Politics

Earlier in the day we had a conference at HQ, or rather a lecture from one of the Intelligence Officers on the political background and the latest information to reach us from the country we are going to — Greece. It's pretty complicated. I'm quite ignorant about Balkan Politics and Greek history and politics; but it seems the partisans with whom our liaison officers work are not all unified. One group in the West of Greece, called EDES, is under the command of a General Xervas. He seems a fairly sound and trustworthy type; but has little or no influence on what is done in the rest of Greece where a large partisan movement, called EAM, operates. As far as I could follow it this EAM is a political organization and has a guerrilla army called ELAS. EAM also contains the Communist group called KKE. The Patriots, far larger than the Xervas lot, don't seem to have a single leader and nobody quite knows what their intentions are when Greece is 'liberated'. The gen that comes out from our agents — the cloak and dagger boys — is rather confusing. The extent to which the partisans are really harassing the Hun with sabotage, etc. is difficult to assess. Some say they are storing all the arms and ammunition so as to be well stocked up for the civil war that will follow! Some say they have made a pact with the Hun to take over their dumps, in return for which they will let him get out of the country unmolested. The whole situation looks rather as if the Greeks weren't putting up much of a show against the Hun and if ELAS should happen to turn against us it might be awkward.

For we, of course, aren't going to 'invade' Greece, as we invaded Normandy. The Hun is withdrawing everywhere. Our major business in the Med is in Italy — to get our bombers within range of his vital targets. Men and machines can't be spared to mount a major attack where it doesn't matter. All we are going to do is to occupy the country immediately the Hun starts to leave it and, we hope, harass him badly on his way out. We are going in with quite a small force, but most people seem to think that in spite of the cross-currents of internal politics, when our chaps turn up with supplies and food the chances of trouble are negligible. I must say everyone is frightfully cheery and co-operative. There's a sort of picnic atmosphere about it all, and those who know the country well give the impression that before the war the Greeks were tops.

Delays

Everybody's getting fed up with hanging about. We are all set to go, but the Hun won't oblige by leaving Athens, so the whole thing hangs fire. This has led to a change of plan — one of those alterations I told you about earlier that makes the Movements Officer go crazy. We have information that the Hun is pretty well out of the Peloponnese already and there's an airfield at its western tip, at the entrance to the Gulf of Corinth, called Araxos from which we could operate against the retreating enemy. So we've signalled our local agent to get the airfield serviceable as quick as he can (it's full of craters at the moment) and meanwhile we are sending down a flight of Spits to operate from an improvised landing strip nearby. All this is nothing to do with me but the AOC wants some of my men, my Flight Control Officers, Fitters, Riggers and so on. I have to reorganize my sea party, which has already left for Taranto. Luckily, I have a very steady officer, called Stockall, to put in charge of the show and the idea is that when we do make Athens they all pack up at Araxos and join us. Meanwhile it means recalling some men and officers, replacing them with others, resorting kit, etc, etc.

Night Landing

The Spits went in a couple of days ago, but Signals seem to be having some difficulty getting them, so HQ don't quite know what's going on. Bob Fokey suggested to the AOC that I should nip down with the Dakotas (who are nightly taking supplies into the Spits) and report progress. I took it as rather a compliment that the idea was agreed to, since I'm not a member of the Operations Command.

An atmosphere of excitement and tension, inseparable from Ops, hung round the Briefing Room of the Transport Squadron. They are a wonderful crowd, led by a man from Kenya. I have been living in their Mess for the last few days and getting to know them pretty well. Nightly for months they have been penetrating deep into enemy country carrying supplies to aid the guerrillas in Yugoslavia, Italy, Greece. Sometimes they drop them by parachute, sometimes they land on specially prepared 'strips'. Landing is a tricky business for they have to make hurried getaways if Hun patrols spot where they have come down. They bring back prisoners or spies or wounded men. Every night when they return they come in for debriefing and have stories to tell and valuable information to give.

But of course the run down to Araxos was a picnic. Three aircraft were detailed for the trip and, after supper, I took off with the first. It was overcast as we went south to take our departure from the heel of Italy, but cleared as we crossed the Adriatic and made our landing on the islands that guard the entrance to the Gulf of Cornith. The golden pathway on the sea below made by the rising moon showed the islands in a silhouette of jet against the water. I was up in the cockpit with the crew most of the trip and we could see the flarepath on the landing strip from miles away.

We circled and landed in the dewy grass and were welcomed by the WingCo in charge. A rabble of Greeks with carts came to help in the unloading. My chaps in the sea party haven't arrived yet, but one or two who were flown in seemed cheery and contented, though they complained of the mosquitoes! I had a chat with the WingCo, cleared the Signals difficulty, took a long list of wanted stores and in half an hour we were off again and back in the Mess an hour and a half later. I enjoyed the trip. It was somehow romantic and mysterious, though quite without incident — except that the second aircraft hit a horse on landing and the Greek owner, cap in hand, came asking compensation for the horse — and the foal it was carrying!

Standing By

But today it started to rain in torrents. The landing strip the Spits are using is really the bed of a dried-up lake, so they are likely to be bogged down at once.

In fact an aircraft that went down to reconnoitre saw them making frantic efforts to get the Spits away before they are irretrievably stuck. However, Araxos proper should be serviceable in a day or two, though the Hun shows no sign of leaving Patras, sixteen miles away, where is more or less besieged by the local guerrillas.

Meanwhile the operation still hangs fire. Everybody is getting nervy at standing by, particularly the airborne crowd who are living a bit further south in bivouac tents — no joke in this sort of weather. The rain is really something. The dried-up stream beds around Bari are rushing torrents of brown water, the roads are flooded, the airfield is unserviceable — a mush of brown mud. Everyone is depressed.

Crisis

I don't expect you thought you'd get a letter from Cairo, but two things have happened — both out of the blue, First, Greek D-Day has been unexpectedly delayed, then my backside trouble, which I told you was still hanging about, suddenly blew up. AOC thought it wouldn't be a good idea to go into Greece, where there might be very little medical help available, if I could get something done first. The delay seemed a golden opportunity for me to nip down to the Delta and deal with it. So he started making signals. I flew down and now I've got it all behind me (literally!) before the new D-Day comes up.

I must say the medics were awfully good. I was in and out of the hospital in three days. I had a chance to check up with all my officers and men coming out of the Delta. The new D-Day has given me a couple of days rest and now, instead of getting on board an aircraft in Bari, I'll be getting on one here and touch down in Athens with the first wave. It's all worked out perfectly.

The Liberators

It is 14 October and we have 'liberated' Greece! Night has fallen and I am sitting in a hotel bedroom in the heart of Athens. The window is open and through it, high above, I can see the light that crowns the tiny shrine of Mount Lycabettus. From below comes a mutter of joy. It wells up from the brightly lit streets — for the Hun seems to have left the power stations intact — where processions pass carrying banners and singing. The whole city is a flutter of flags. One wonders where did they manage to hide them. They hang from the housefronts, literally in hundreds. It is like a Carnival. The whole of Greece seems to be in the streets, singing and cheering and applauding as we pass, throwing flowers at our lorries and surrounding every stationary group of men. I suppose they remember the tragic days in 1941 when we came to their help only to beat a hasty retreat ourselves! They have longed for our return. Well, here we are!

It makes me feel a bit awkward for, though I suppose we do represent victory, I can't somehow see myself as a hero. Actually I feel a bit whacked. Up since 3 a.m. It's been quite a day, with everyone a bit inclined to stand on their heads; but we've made it. That's the great thing, and we've received such a welcome as I shall never forget. But I'd better begin at the beginning.

When we entered the Aegean and the last hour of our trip began the views grew quite fairylike. You must sometimes get fed up with the way I go on, but I do seem to have the most extraordinary luck when I see things for the first time. All around us were gaunt islands, lying about in the aquamarine sea like lumps of pumice stone. The sea was so still that each island was reflected in it and, due to some convection effect, each was also crowned with a circlet of cloud, a wreath of white, now rosy in the morning sun. These airy diadems were also reflected in the water, so there were islands and cloud islands, reflections and cloud reflections, all so mazed and intermingled that it was difficult to believe the whole scene was no more than the 'baseless fabric of a vision'.

On all this, as we made our approach, the sun shone, olives glistened and the little island fishing ports were tucked snugly into their bays, seeming to invite the sailors home. There was an electric feeling of joy in the air, heightened I'm sure by the sense of occasion, the approach to the immortal city, white across the bay, backed by its gaunt hills, Hymettus, and Pentelikon, and the misty stretch of the plains of Attica. The sky was full of aircraft circling to come in to land and on the airfield below great activity as freight and troop carriers disgorged their loads.

I found that my seaborne party had arrived during the night. Richardson, my Traffic Officer, had wandered round the airfield in the dark, expecting to be blown up by landmines at any moment, but had found a billet in a disused hangar, settled the men in, got the cookhouse going, erected a couple of tents and waded into his job. Excellent! Though everyone is spinning a bit, the plans are all working out as we hoped and everything is under control.

Later in the day a lot of us crowded into a jeep to go up to the city. The road runs along the coast, past scattered groups of little villas and small hotels as far as Phaleron Bay. All along the road people cheered and waved as we passed and then we turned into the magnificent double carriageway that runs from the sea up a five-mile stretch into the city. It is dead straight and as you drive along it you see the whole panorama before you, the Acropolis on your left, Lycabettus ahead, Mount Hymettus on the right and, closing the vista at the end of the way, the tall white pillars of the Temple of Jupiter. I suppose no city has a more magnificent approach. We drove to the hotel allotted to us and managed to get a room for the officers and a meal of bully and biscuits.

I have just been out for a stroll. The whole city is in the streets. Crowds throng everywhere, the buildings are floodlit, processions pass, singing, and we are cheered wherever we go. People come up and wring your hand and talk away quite oblivious that you can't understand a word! Loudspeakers are relaying political speeches, the whole place is one big smile. This is the moment of joy, freedom, liberation. Impossible to describe — but impossible to forget.

Billets

I have had an immensely full day. But such a beautiful, crystalline day to get my first taste of Greece, so full of warm sunshine, blue sea and noble views over mountains and bays, I am quite in love with the place already. Seeing everything was going smoothly on the field I left that to look after itself and started out to find billets for the men.

The place I made for is a villa suburb, Kifissia, some eight miles outside the city on the lower slopes of Mount Pentelikon, from which the marble for the Acropolis was quarried. There are still big white gashes on the slopes. When I reached the place it was to find it among pinewoods, pinewoods smelling more richly and sweetly than any I have known elsewhere — that wonderful healthy smell of resin which makes you breathe deep to savour it.

Without much trouble I found quite a decent hotel for the men, a villa for the Sergeants' Mess and another for ourselves — so palatial and with such marble bathrooms I feel I shall have to give parties in my bath! We shall be comfortable, too comfortable and, back of it all, I always have the feeling that we are, if not enjoying it, at least having an easy time out here while you at home are being bombed and rocketed and kept on short commons. We are further from it all than you are and there is little or no sense of urgency. I suppose someone must look after the lines of communication and though I am quite certain that my work, and that of all my chaps, is efficiently done, I don't really feel happy in the comfort that we have.

Hospitality

As we were setting out on our billet hunt a Greek came up and spoke to me. He had lived for many years in Cardiff, owned eighteen ships, every one of which had been sunk during the war! He insisted on becoming our guide and finding us what we wanted. The first place he took us to I knew was no good before we got there, but it belonged to some friends of his and we had to go in out of courtesy.

The door was opened by a smiling white-haired man who only spoke French but he insisted that we come in and drink a cup of Turkish coffee. I protested that we were busy, for I knew what they had all been through and didn't like to accept their hospitality, but there was no getting out of it, for I could see they would have been offended, so we sat and chatted while the daughter of the house, a plain, plump girl with a beaming smile, produced delicious preserved cherries in white syrup on a tray with a glass of kummel and another of water. I felt ashamed to take these things which had obviously been stored for some special occasion. I suppose the arrival of the British was such an occasion, but when this was followed up with beautiful sweet coffee, Turkish cigarettes and, when we rose to leave at last, with big bouquets of white roses for myself and the officer who was with me, I was touched beyond measure. It so obviously came from the heart. Liberty means something here. It is not a political slogan on a hoarding, but a wonderful, unbelievable relief. It makes one feel that the war has not been fought in vain. I hope the feeling will not fade.

Cocktail Party

Writing at 7 am. Perfect madhouse yesterday, scrounging furniture, desks, beds, etc, etc, for the men and officers. Every man will have a bed, a spring mattress and a wardrobe, all in a decent hotel. They are delighted and say they have never known anything like it since they came overseas. I got this stuff from the abandoned German Air Force HQ. Nothing like being first in the field! We haven't, of course, taken anything from the Greeks.

When the day's rush was over I went on to a cocktail party, quiet and pleasant, rather like one at home. I had had breakfast at seven, biscuits and dripping for lunch, no tea, but when they started handing round things to eat, I felt I couldn't touch them and fed them to whichever girl I happened to be talking to.

They couldn't think why, or so pretended, but after all, it's the limit to come to a starving country and eat their food.

While waiting to be picked up, I went for a stroll in the square near our hotel. It was falling dusk, a lemon sky with a sickle moon, crowds in the streets, loudspeakers relaying speeches and a sort of buzz and bubble of happiness in the air. I sat for a little at an open air cafe to drink a glass of ouzo, the local absinthe which, on my empty tummy, made me a bit squiffy. I watched the people passing. Occasionally you may see the classic features of the statues, but mostly they are dark and rather hairy! No wonderful looks or wonderful figures, but something, I don't know what, awfully English about them! I never understood the traditional friendship between the two countries before, but now I do. They seem to have something of the same outlook, forthright, sophisticated, adult — and just now they are so happy it is a pleasure to look at their faces. Well, now to breakfast. And am I hungry after my fast yesterday!

Tatoi

Long before we came to Greece it was decided that, as soon as possible, I should move from the 'operational' field by the coast, Hassani, where the Beaufighters and Spits are to be stationed, and be responsible for all the non-operational aircraft on my own airfield — the old commercial one, situated eight miles north of Athens, near the royal Summer Palace, and called Tatoi. In the course of getting billets for the men up at Kifissia I went to see Tatoi which is another eight miles from Kifissia.

Nothing is so depressing as the devastation of a blitzed site. As I stood on Tatoi airfield and saw the piles of fallen masonry, the huge water towers lying prone, the tangled wreckage of steel girders that had been hangars, the shells of buildings less windows and glass, I saw the old job ahead, patching and scrounging, coaxing and cajoling and pushing, pushing, pushing to get all our requirements met. I shall need electric light and telephones and water, carpenters, masons, and labourers. I shall have to arrange for mine-detector squads to go over the roads and runways and dispersal areas. We shall want tractors, bull-dozers, scrapers and, before we start I know supplies will be short and the REs will have a dozen other jobs as urgent as ours. Generally speaking the Hun hasn't gone far in carrying out his scorched earth policy in Greece, except at the airfields. Tatoi is a shambles. However, the REs are a very good lot and I think in a week or two, we should be able to have the place operational.

In all this I have been given the greatest assistance by the old pre-war Manager of BOAC (British Overseas Airways Corpn) in Athens, a man called Lagopoulos. He came up to me the first day we arrived and, speaking perfect English, asked if I could tell him anything about his old firm. Would they be starting a service to Athens again, could he get in touch with them, and so on. When I told him that until the end of hostilities Trans-port Command was BOAC, he was delighted, attached himself to me, and has been a tower of strength and help ever since. He knows the ropes, acts as interpreter and is fast becoming guide, philosopher and friend. He has produced some of his old staff, drivers, fitters and clerks, to say nothing of cars, type-writers, etc — all very useful just now until our stuff arrives.

The stories he tells of the occupation are endless. He was an active member of the underground association that helped many of our chaps get away. He had British officers in his house for months and hairbreadth escapes from being discovered by the Huns.

Money

Our occupation of Greece doesn't seem to be working out according to plan. Intelligence don't seem to have done their homework, for the Piraeus which was to receive all our sea-borne forces turns out to be far more seriously damaged than we anticipated, with the result that all unloading schedules are way behind. All reinforcements are delayed. My own party should have been here by now and there isn't a sign of it. All the other units are in the same state so my ten three-tonners have had to help out all round. The wretched drivers are having to work 15 hours a day. We can't go on long at this rate, but there's a splendid spirit everywhere, which alone makes it possible.

It isn't only the failure of the unloading schedules. Essentials are missing. There is no bread or meat! We are all living on emergency rations. Bully beef and biscuits and boiled sweets! Some basics have been forgotten altogether. For instance, there is no money! No rate of exchange has been arranged between the pound and the drachma. British Military Currency has no status — and anyway, there isn't any! Nobody has sent it in!

The drachma is worthless. Lagopoulos gave me a set of notes today ranging from a few drachmas to 200 billion. And this is hardly enough to buy a slice of bread. Cigarettes are three million drachmas each! Prices and wages are still soaring in the approved manner, while there is bread on sale in the streets and vegetables, fruit and cakes — if you are a millionaire. The only worthwhile currency is the Gold Pound — for our people used this, while the enemy was in the country, to pay for services rendered. It stands at about five to the paper pound, but nobody has any paper pounds so that doesn't help much!

No doubt this will all be straightened out, but one wonders who is responsible for flagrant omissions of this kind. It is the same thing I noticed in Sicily — the 'liberators', after all their propaganda, turn up badly organized and unable to carry out their promises. It makes me ashamed when I can't pay for hired cars or give wages to those who have helped us. However, the general feeling of co-operation and good will is so great that it doesn't seem to make any difference — so far.

Sometimes remarks made by the Greeks are really touching. Today, when Lagopoulos was having 'lunch' with me, which consisted of soup, bread, marge, jam and a piece of chocolate, he said, 'D'you know, this is the first real meal I've had in four years.'

Warning Slogans

Greece is a gaunt romantic country, bare mountains and blue sea. But I think the most wonderful thing about it is the light. It is incredibly polished and lucid. I feel I can see further and more clearly here than I have ever seen before. There is a sort of diamond quality about it, as if the outline of everything was etched in sparkling brilliance. Perhaps it is the time of year, warm days and nights very clean, cool and threatening cold, with the promised sharp Greek winter not far away.

Walking about the town the most noticeable thing is the way slogans are daubed all over the place in red paint. These vary from 'Welcome to our Brave Allies' to 'Hello, Tommy, glad to see you!' — but they are all invariably signed EAM or ELAS and decorated with the hammer and sickle. I don't know how patriotic this guerrilla movement is, but they certainly have a good eye for propaganda — with a sort of hint of a threat in it. However, whatever political developments there may be, for the moment everything goes smoothly and we get almost embarrassing welcomes wherever we go.

Back To Hassani

I am absolutely fed up today! After working myself and the whole unit silly, I managed to open up Tatoi in three weeks! The REs played up wonderfully, some more transport and light-ing vehicles arrived, we managed to get glass into the windows and the telephones working and a hundred and one other jobs done. It was quite an effort, considering the state the field was in. I even got buses running for passengers and opened up a snack bar!

And then Whitney arrives, takes one look at the Tatoi, pronounces it impossible as a permanent site for civil aircraft, goes off to see the AOC, Tuttle, who agrees that the needs of operational aircraft are now much less (the Hun having got out of Greece double quick) and there is no reason why I should not be on the same field with the operational units, and orders me back to Hassani!

So all our work has been for nothing. And the RE's work too. I shall have to find new billets for officers and men, right on the other side of Athens, now, when other units have got the best accommodation. I shall have, in fact, to start all over again!

Mind you I think it was the right decision. Hassani has a runway. I didn't have the experience and didn't see, as Whitney did at once, that the gravel surface at Tatoi would rip the tyres off transport aircraft in a couple of landings. I only wish he'd come by earlier, that's all.

The worst of it is that I'd promised myself I'd get really good billets for the whole unit for the winter — and now we can't possibly hang on to our hotel at Kifissia. Much too far to move the men to work. And there's nothing, absolutely nothing, at Hassani. No offices, stores, workshops, etc. The Staging Post is quite a big set-up. I shall have to find huts, build them probably, and wood is frightfully scarce in Greece. It can't be done under a month, so we shall have to hang on to things as they are until then.

Besides, of course, the first flush of all-out co-operation is finished. Routine, the usual channels, permissions, authorities etc, are beginning to raise their paralysing influence and slow everything up. Oh, damn it all!

Victory Parade

The glorious autumn days are over. We have been in Greece over a month. December is approaching. Chill winds blow down from the mountains. Somehow the splendour of the first days seems to have evaporated. I suppose it was inevitable. The liberation has not produced the millennium overnight. The Greeks are just beginning to realize it — and we are just beginning to realize the strength of the political undercurrents that flow beneath the apparently carefree surface. I wonder how it will all go.

Everybody assumes that 'things' will be arranged on the political side. But I saw a procession several miles long in Athens two days ago. It was a Victory Parade, staged by EAM — and a tacit demonstration of power. Most of the young men and girls with their guns, bandoliers and banners looked bored and sheepish, but some were fierce and violent-looking. Perhaps the pessimists are right — we ARE sitting on a volcano! The eruption will come, no doubt, when the AOC Greece, General Scobie, tells the 'freedom fighters' to lay down their arms. Will they? They have sidestepped the issue so far, but it can't be delayed for ever.

Shepherd's Delight

Today I haven't much to tell you about really — except an extremely hectic party given by certain members of our Diplomatic Corps who shall be nameless!

One of them knew a Taverna out in the country run by a Greek who rejoiced in the name of Peter Christos. So we set out in two cars for this place which lay some twenty miles outside Athens over the worst roads ever. At the end of it, rather shaken, we pulled up at a low white building standing absolutely alone in the deserted countryside. Inside we found a big white empty room, lit by one acetylene flare.

Some shepherds sat huddled in a corner by a bare wooden table and I began to wonder what sort of a place we had got ourselves into. We were about twelve strong, including two Embassy cypherenes, Bob and I representing the RAF and the rest were all 'diplomatists' I hope! We were to be joined by the

Big Noise, irreverently known by his staff as the High Purge; but he didn't turn up. However, the retsina did.

It came in big jugs. Very cold and a good foil to the crisp dry cabbage hearts, radishes and olives which came with it. Next appeared small fish which we ate whole and later some spaghetti with bits of small birds in it — very tasty. The food kept coming along in a desultory sort of way, but the wine came along much faster.

Then a guitarist appeared. He played really well and, bit by bit, the shepherds joined us and we all began to sing. Greek songs are sad and strange, something like flamenco, with the same whole tone scale, the same short strophes, the same melodious link for the guitarist alone between the bursts of singing. There were songs that might have been about raiding and adventure, others about love and longing, all of them had something that pulled at the heart, a sort of loneliness, a falling cadence which seemed to have been created at that moment, a spontaneous improvisation conceived to catch us as we felt then — a quality the West has almost entirely lost. Only Chopin, I suppose, catches that spontaneous rush of something brand new, just created. I have heard stories of parties — in Persia, I believe — where the guest of honour suggests the subject for a poem, which a poet creates there and then and to which a guitarist improvises the accompaniment.

Anyway whether it was the retsina or the emotional state the Greeks were in — and we too — lifted by the new-found liberty of Greece, I found the music wonderful, dark and passionate, wild and gay, rooted in the Turk, the Saracen, the Moor, the people who have flooded into Attica ever since the Golden Age faded.

When I do get drunk, which isn't very often, I do like it to be on wine and in congenial company. As the evening progressed, I was told afterwards, I turned into the life and soul of the party and my rendering of 'My old man's a fireman, Now what d'you think of that?' was a smash hit. Later, when Bob and I executed a riotous pas de deux, we established for ever the RAF's right to be considered the senior service in Greece.

We didn't get back till three and today I feel terrible!

The Wood Cutters

Somehow, from the airfield, the sea looks colder and more sombre now it is overcast. The mountains are still clear of snow, but icy winds blow down from Thebes and the golden tints of the forests round the Royal Palace, just north of Tatoi, have suddenly disappeared. On the roads leading to them you can see the reason — thousands and thousands of handcarts and perambulators loaded to overflowing with wood!

With no laws, no police protection and no effective means of control, there is nothing to stop the mass destruction of the forests. This afternoon I counted 450 carts on a five-mile stretch of road! The price is £8 for as much wood as you can get in a small perambulator. All day and night the pillage goes on. Stretches of road that were shaded one day are bare the next. Little urchins and old men, women and girls, they are all out on the road in their thousands, pushing or dragging the little carts.

True, as the AOC said, 'Better a warm Greek than a cold one', but knowing the effect that denuding the countryside has on climate, looking up to the mountains all round us here that were once dark with forests of pine and are now gaunt skeletons; it's a dismal sight, one further step in the impoverishment of Greece and tragic to see the Greeks taking it themselves. But when people are faced with cold and hunger ...

The Unknown Warrior

We are back to days of incredible visibility, magnificent sunsets and glittering starlit nights. The AOC noticed the low crescent moon with a big star over the bow and remarked that it only needed a hammer and sickle to make the sky communist! It made us laugh for the city is scrawled all over with these slogans. A few days ago was Greek Armistice Day and the night before ELAS and KKE gangs splashed their grafitti all over the stairways leading down to the Tomb! Really! As soon as the day broke and their work was seen, rival factions set to work with mop and broom and washed them all off again! How can you take such pranks seriously? But it is just one more sign that the situation is deteriorating. Everybody is a bit on edge. Nobody quite knows what ELAS will do when their bluff is called.

The Unknown Warrior's Tomb in Athens is set in the wall of a terrace on which stands a building that used to be the Royal Palace. It is a nice large stucco house, not at all pretentious, but of simple and dignified proportions. Cream-washed with green-shuttered windows, it stands on a high ground and at either end flights of steps lead down to a paved open space below. Beyond is the main road.

Inset into the terrace wall between the two descending flights of steps is a bas relief of white marble, a nude warrior wearing a Greek helmet. It is a fine design. Below this plaque is the Tomb which is guarded night and day by the Royal Guards in their lovely uniforms — white tights, short white cloaks overlaid with lace, scarlet berets, white hose and black slippers with enormous bobbles on the toes. Two Guards stand before sentry boxes either side of the Tomb. These sentry boxes are also white and have tilted canvas shades over them, in blue and white stripes — the Greek national colours — to keep off the sun. There is something simple and touching about the whole thing. When I saw it I remembered how in the days of old the Greeks always had this informal attitude towards things which were sacred to them. Their gods were not inaccessible, omnipotent and terrible. They were, so to speak, just over lifesize and were subject to human weaknesses and emotions. Perhaps they were more easily loved for that.

The Tomb is situated right in the centre of the city, with hotels, blocks of flats and public buildings around. On this morning, the first celebration of the day since the war, the streets were thronged with thousands of people. It was a National Holiday and the bright sun and cloudless sky lent a natural gaiety to the scene. Detachments of troops lined the roads and the approaches. There was a group of those whose sons had fallen in the War. These stood near the Tomb and waited for the distinguished persons and priests to arrive.

For half an hour, before anything began to happen, processions of young people swung across the terrace below (where I stood with other officers looking down on the whole scene) chanting short staccato phrases, which I understood to mean 'Long Live Greece!' These were repeated time after time and mingled with bursts of frenzied cheering as the 'great' began to arrive. Ambassadors, Generals, Scobie (who got a roar from the crowd who seem to adore him) and, of course, our Geoffrey, took their places and were followed by the Bishops and Archbishops of the Greek Orthodox Church in their flowing black robes, some in sumptuous embroidered stoles and all with their inverted top hats and veils and sporting gorgeous beards!

There wasn't much solemnity about the ceremony. Odd people slipped through the police cordon and wandered about, little children ran for leaflets which formations of aircraft let drop. They came fluttering down like a cloud of white doves and the children ran for them. At intervals there was silence as wreaths were laid and a trumpet blew clear and short. Then it was over and the march Past began and we all relaxed and lit cigarettes and chatted to the Greek officers with us. It was a curious ceremony. It should have been solemn yet it was uncontrollably gay. I could not help contrasting it with our own, on the 11th. Then there was true solemnity. The public respected our mood and not a soul moved in that open space. It was so broad and sombre. 'Time like an ever-rolling stream, Bears all its sons away ...' I can hardly hear that tune without a catch at the throat, it moves me so, carrying me back to cold, grey Whitehall, packed with people, to the wheeling pigeons in the silence after Big Ben has struck, carrying me back to my youth, to friends long dead but still remembered, carrying me back to England and to you.

Politics

I had a long talk with one of our Greek Liaison Officers today. In half an hour he gave me more of a picture of our situation in Greece than I've got from all the conferences.

When we withdrew (rather hurriedly) in 1941, the speed and violence of the German advance left the Greeks quite stunned. When they rallied it was to try to form some common national resistance to hinder and harass, by every possible means, the enemy who had occupied their country.

But how to go about it? They had no idea, nothing whatever to build on. It was then that the Communists (KKE) came forward and offered to place their own excellent organization, comprising cells throughout Greece (and a lot of underground communications), at the disposal of the combined parties.

But since politics is the Greek national sport and as two Greeks appear unable to agree on anything for more than five minutes, the common front soon began to split up. After the usual endless talk, it finally settled into two parties: the Royalists, nationalists, conservatives, called EDES, and the Communists, called EAM — far more aggressive and soon quite a considerable and active force. They quickly developed a fighting arm, and it is these guerrillas — now well equiped with the arms we have dropped duirng the occupation! — that call themselves ELAS, daub their slogans all over the place and hope to take over the government of Greece.

There are a few other factors on the sidelines — those who managed to get away and formed themselves into the Royal Greek Hellenic Air Force, also a small nucleus of a Greek Army and the remnants of the Greek Navy, who joined up with ours. Besides them there is also the Provisional Government, formed by Eden in 1942, which came in with the rest of us from Egypt and is now supposed to be running the country.

Of course it has always been the Allied policy to develop underground resistance movements by peppering 'occupied territories' with 'liaison officers', highly trained men, skilled in sabotage and propaganda. Here in Greece they have been a great success, but of course they have left a legacy (which we were bound to ignore at the time): large dumps of arms and ammunition scatterd all over the country in the hands of half-organized soldiery. If these people grow restive and disagree with their country's policy they may constitute quite a threat to internal peace. This is exactly that situation which seems to be developing here.

But beyond this there is another factor which is only now just begining to surface: we have fanned resistance movements for our own ends; but what about national ends? Resistance may well have its own patriotic and political ideologies. Men who take great risks naturally claim a share in shaping their country's destiny when the fighting is over. But since we have fought for democratic principles and the right of all countries to choose their own form of government in free elections, we are certainly not going to let the local Communists, ELAS, take over the government of Greece at gunpoint.

But how do you hold free elections? The provisional government has no authority. All the communications through which government governs — roads, railways, telephones — are non-existent. You cannot begin to organize elections. The state of the country is chaotic. If elections were to be held now, they would be forced elections with ELAS Tommy guns in the backs of the electors.

So here we are, trying to keep the peace, in a situation growing steadily worse and, if it comes to a showdown, without sufficient forces to hold off the local gangsters — for that is what it amounts to.

I can't help feeling here, as I did in Sicily, the extraordinary lack of forethought and planning in the whole operation. The information was available long before we came in; but Intelligence was ignored, we didn't want to spare the troops, so we just pressed on, trusted to luck and here we are! Well maybe that was justified in 1941 — but not now. My friend the liaison officer had been working with ELAS for over a year. He was quite sure we were in for civil war; but the general opinion seems incurably optimistic. Nobody takes the thing seriously.

And you can see why! There is something so wonderful about the place, about the atmosphere. One simply can't believe in conflict, bloodshed, in this setting. Earlier this evening I went round to the little fishing port again, borrowed a dory and rowed round among the caiques, floating so still at anchor on the evening water. The sun set on Hymettus, washing it all deep violet. I sat and drank a glass of ouzo with the fishermen. Many were taking their evening meal in the open air on the quayside, very simple and happy. It was all masts and shrouds and hanging nets and the silhouette of sails in the offing. Heavenly! I had been full of worries, but here I was at once calmed and refreshed and returned in a wonderful humour to write to you!

Partisans

Although we were ordered back to Hassani (the main airport) we haven't moved there yet. The men are still in their splendid accommodation at Kifissia and all our vehicles, petrol bowsers, radio lorries, etc. are at Tatoi. The main trouble is moving people about. It is about 8 miles from Tatoi to Kifissia and about the same from Kifissia to Hassani and we never seem to have enough transport. All aircraft visiting Athens land at Hassani. So we must have a party of some kind working there to service, refuel them, etc. But where to put them? There's no accommodation whatever. I've managed to get hold of a couple of huts, but they aren't erected yet and the so-called carpenters have only one tool!

I must say it's a wonderful tool, a sort of hammer-cum-axe-cum-nail-extractor and they use it with great skill, bashing, paring, shaping, chopping — and hanging it over their shoulder when they need to have two hands free! It's cold now, but they seem oblivious of the temperature and work away cheerfully enough, but every now and then they get orders and just disappear, ordered off the job, by whom, for what reason? Nobody knows. It is this that produces the state of tension. It makes me feel quite impotent. I don't speak a word of Greek and there is this sort of nebulous power, unseen, in the background, controlling what I can and cannot do. I don't like it!

There are heavily armed ELAS men all over the place too. They're not at all belligerent, just wandering about, watching, talking, smoking. Only yesterday we picked one up on the road. He wanted a lift into town. He really was a gorgeous ruffian with a shiny Sten gun, two crossed bandoliers full of ammo, an automatic at his hip, two big knives in his belt, breeches, putties, a great black beard and a cheerful grin! But, all the same, he was heavily armed — and I haven't worn a firearm since I arrived!

It set me thinking. Who was the man? Where had he come from? How did he acquire all those weapons? We have a few English-speaking Greeks working with us and I talked with them, trying to understand it all better.

The partisan, the young man who goes off to the mountains to escape the law and fight for 'freedom', and who is prepared to live a spartan life to get it, all this is in the Greek tradition, extant long prior to the war, or even the century, for Greece lived for many years under the dominion of the Turks. So there is every reason to expect a general sympathy with the partisan. But it doesn't seem the present lot are at all popular. Indeed the peasants are said to go in terror of them. They terrify the starving countryside and live off it, looting and murdering, utterly irresponsible and undisciplined. I wonder if it is true?

These girls and boys of seventeen and eighteen were no more than children when the Hun came in. They lost all chance of education, all home influence, they fled to the mountains to escape the forced labour gangs, they lived like animals. War was a licence for lust, theft and murder. It was easy to destroy — and fun. They were brought up to it. Most of them have never dreamed of living a peaceful life or studying to work or make a living; all they can do is use a gun. They have been well paid for it too. But now the pay has stopped and, what is more, we are asking them to return the gun! The only tool they can use, their only capital asset!

So, all ideology apart, ELAS stick together. Their leaders want to seize power and the rank and file to seize food, property or anything else they happen to fancy. So when we tell them that those days are over, that they must go back to their villages, lay down their arms, till the soil and Long Live Greece, it doesn't exactly go with a swing. Still, there can't be any internal security in Greece till these young fanatics are disarmed.

As the days go by, this situation is moving to its climax. EAM keep putting off the day. We continue to be wonderfully patient. but I fancy they are construing this as weakness, multiplying their demands and getting steadily more truculent. They now demand every key post in the government as the price of co-operation. Scobie, Macmillan* and Leeper† are working on it night and day, but the situation is steadily deteriorating. The Xervas lot now say they won't disarm till ELAS do — they know they'd be murdered if they did! What an aftermath!

Night Out

In the middle of all this I was invited out to a Taverna supper by a Greek Wing Commander. We picked up some other people and the whole party proceeded straight to the kitchen — I understand it's the usual Greek custom to go and see the food and

---

*Harold Macmillan, later Prime Minister and Earl of Stockton, was Minister Resident at Allied HQ in North-West Africa, 1942-45.
† Sir Rex Leeper, British Ambassador to Greece.

choose what to have. There turned out to be fresh pork, liver and little fishes. After that we went and sat on uncomfortable chairs at a bare table in an empty room — and waited! Except for two or three people drinking in a far corner there were no other diners.

After a bit some ouzo, cabbage hearts and olives appeared and the orchestra — two guitars and a zymbalom — started to strum away in the background. When we'd bought them a round of drinks things began to warm up a bit and one of the guitarists, a very good looking young man, opened his mouth and sang! I was quite unprepared for the natural beauty of his voice. We begged him to come over to our table and soon everyone began to join in. One of the girls, Rena, had a fine voice and everybody sang parts. How different it was from anything at home! These people all sang naturally, sang and sang and sang, seeming to know the words and tunes of innumerable songs. Some of them were rhythmic, martial, vigorous, some sentimental, some queer and oriental and most of them exquisite — or so I thought as the evening wore on and the wine went round.

What is there about these evenings that I shall never forget? A bare room, garish light, rickety chairs, scraps of food and everybody talking gibberish — as far as I was concerned! And yet, and yet … Within an hour, strangers joining up to make one table, all coming together in the singing, in a feeling of joy, happiness and friendship at being with people you'd never met and didn't know, of being carried away by strange and beautiful music that called up such emotions of tenderness, sorrow, wonder and hope that nothing would ever be the same again. You couldn't understand the words, you would forget the tunes, it would all dissolve in the very act of being created — but it was unique, the spirit of Greece of those first days of freedom, when they had come through.

It all broke up about midnight and I went back to bed. But when I saw the Greek Wing Comander this morning, he was wearing summer drill. As the weather was now jolly cold, I thought it was a bit funny and asked him why. I wish I could reproduce his answer, the droll accent, the charm. He is a small smiling man. He looks as if you ought to glue his feet together and stick him on a bottle. He said:

'Lewis, things, unimaginable things, happen to me — you would not believe. I was to take Ellie (one of the girls) home; but she said: Let us go down to the sea and look at the moon. So we drove down to the sea and looked at the moon and she said: It would be nice to go out in a boat. Now you cannot imagine there would be a boat, there at the roadside but when we got out of the car, there, sure enough, was a boat. But a very small boat, a boat with a flat bottom and Ellie said: Let us go for a row. She is crazy you know, but crazy. So I said: Listen, Ellie, it is two o'clock in the morning and that boat is for one, it is not for two. So she said: So you are afraid, are you? — so we got in the boat. And when we were in the boat and I pulled the oars, happened what I knew would happen, the boat turned over. And there we were in the water — and it was cold. So we swam ashore and climbed out. And there we were, dripping wet and nobody, luckily, to see us. So we could not sit in the car dripping wet like that. So Ellie said: Let us take off our clothes and put them in the boot. So when we were quite naked we got in the car and drove back. But I thought: Now, if anyone should stop us and see two naked people driving right through the centre of Athens, this would be a scandal — and I an Air Ministry Official! But we got home safely and I have no other uniform but this drill and that is why I am wearing it.'

Air Traffic

Down in Cairo before we started up this show everybody poo-poohed the importance of Athens. It was a sideshow. A couple of services down to Cairo, a couple up to Bari, maybe a weekly run to Bucharest and that's it. Never more than five aircraft a day. 'It's a piece of cake, old boy,' they said. 'Nothing to do and a nice spot to do it in.'

We have now been here over six weeks and our average daily landings are thirty plus! And it shows no sign of letting up. People pour in from all over the place. The confused political situation brings all sorts of bigwigs on special missions. The Americans turn up in droves, en route for Bucharest (where cameras are cheap!). Visitors come to see the sights. Although all my men and equipment have turned up now, we are having a tough time keeping up with it all.

There is, of, course, no way of getting about in Greece. All the roads are ruined, all railways damaged beyond repair. (The REs tell me there are two serviceable locomotives in Greece and estimate ten years to get the railways running again.) We are starting up a local air service to Salonika — an hour by air, four days by jeep! Possibly other services will follow. There are to be Greek Internal Air Services, run by Greeks — and I have been given the job, among other things, of initiating training schemes to teach them the mysteries of air line management. As if I knew! I am also sending a detached flight down to Crete, where the Hun has left the island clear, except the extreme western tip, where he is well dug in and may remain, as far as one can see, until peace comes.

Still, working in draughty, half-finished buildings with no water, no bulk petrol supply and quite inadequate arrangements for feeding both staff and passengers, every day is one long series of improvisations. We should never get through it at all if I hadn't a wonderful team of officers and a splendid lot of men.

But it isn't only within the Unit that we get this co-operation. Our AOC, Air Commodore Geoffrey Tuttle, is the best CO I ever worked for. Always alert, vigorous and cordial, his grip on the situation and his habit of treating all adverse situations as if they were a joke excites my admiration and affection. Bob Foley, his senior Staff Officer, his second-in-command, is a perfect foil to him. While Geoffrey is neat, brisk and dapper, Bob is so tall and thin that when he is standing sideways on it is difficult to be sure that he is there! He appears to stroll through life, but it doesn't take long to see that this is simply technique. He comes to us fresh from taking quite a part in mounting the Normandy Invasion, for which he has been awarded the OBE. He knows his staff work and he, and Geoffrey, give me such splendid backing that I would do anything for either of them. Both are also good friends of Whitney Straight, my real boss, so everything goes with a swing!

Problems

The drachma is slipping again, in spite of the bullion we have brought in to peg it at its pre-war level of 600 to the pound. The state of the economy is really chaotic. Until Greece can export she can't get the raw materials necessary to restart her small industrial potential. Her crops of olive oil, raisins, etc, have all been carried off by the Hun and paid for in systematically inflated currency — worthless paper. The ships that could have brought in supplies are at the bottom. Of her pre-war fleet of twelve thousand caiques — the sinews of her inter-island trade — ten thousand have been sunk. Internal trade is at a standstill because of no roads or railways. Motor transport, buses, etc, are in the last stages of decay, no tyres and practically no petrol. Telephones, outside Athens, are a dream of the past — though there was quite a good provincial system before the war.

Altogether it's a pretty bleak prospect. Nobody knows where to begin. The authority of the government runs only where it can reach, that is in Athens and its suburbs. Beyond that it is exercised by the nearest ELAS Tommy gun. Salonika is entirely under ELAS control. Obviously no government can govern in such conditions and no free elections can be held until communications are restored. Heaven knows how long that will take. Sometimes it seems an insoluble situation — and the threats of ELAS only add to the difficulties. They are estimated to number forty thousand, five percent of the population, and their bid to govern Greece, by force if necessary, if it came off, would be just another Nazi-type *coup de main*. When Hitler said he would fight till 'after midnight' I often wonder if the sowing of political chaos was part of the scheme! It won't be long before people are longing for the comparative stability and security of war conditions! Even extortionate government is better than anarchy. At least the evils can be foreseen and to some extent canalized. What a mess! And I'm afraid it's getting worse.

General Strike

I don't like the look of it. Two days ago a general strike was declared. All the labour that had been clearing up at Tatoi and all the carpenters working on our precious huts going up at Hassani, melted away — even leaving their tools on the job. Some of our staff, Greek drivers, clerks and the like, have gone too, but most of them have stuck to us, though they've had some difficulty in getting out to the airfield to work. Yesterday a curfew was imposed and nobody was allowed to go into Athens except on duty. This produced a faint tremor of uneasiness among us all, but still everybody remains incurably optimistic. We don't seem capable of taking the thing seriously. It has all come about, of course, by Scobie finally calling a halt to all the ELAS procrastinations and calling for an immediate laying down of all arms.

This morning the electric power was cut. ELAS have seized the power station. The trams have stopped. The automatic telephone exchange has gone over on to batteries. When these run down, communications will be much impeded, for we haven't many military lines and, being overhead wires, these are easily cut. Our billets up here at Kifissia are a thousand feet above Athens and all water in the district is pumped up electrically. In a few days we shall be out of water. We haven't any water trailers and the wells are poor and few and far between.

I gave orders to get our electric power trailers going to light the men's billets and our own. Nothing so demoralizing as lack of light. The men remain in good spirits. In fact the threat seems to have drawn us closer; but they, like us, remain incurably optimistic. They all have friends among the local Greeks. They are more or less members of the family in many cases and they just can't believe anyone wishes them any harm.

Calm

A most beautiful day today, calm and sunny. The Baron, my old CO from Catania, came through on his way to the UK. After lunch we walked up the lower slopes of Mount Pentelikon, sat on a rise and looked down over the Plain of Attica. Marvellous view. I suppose one of the most inspiring in the world, if you believe in Western Civilization, which was cradled here. We just sat and talked.

There wasn't a sound, nothing moved, the world seemed utterly peaceful and still. I had a curious feeling of being somehow quite outside time. We had a wonderful conversation. Nothing about what was going on. Nothing about war, destruction and death. Just about dreams, hopes, longings, I suppose, for something better, more worthwhile to live for, something to believe in. Strange, with a man I hardly knew, but felt so drawn to.

Then we came down to the Mess and had a drink before he left. Only a glimmer of light. Our homemade power supply can't cope with the load. it was all rather depressing. Waiting for something to happen . . .

. . . Before Storm

I have just finished and posted a reassuring letter to you, but the truth is I am far from reassured myself. The plain facts are that the Staging Post, the entire RAF HQ staff, officers and all personnel are trapped, plainly and obviously trapped, up in our billets at Kifissia.

The thing started about two days back. I was out at Tatoi as usual. An American Colonel had just turned up with a party, with alleged clearance for Bucharest. This is tricky and needs special clearance from Moscow. I was just phoning HQ about this when Bob Foley came through to me.

'Come up here at once. The balloon's gone up.'

'What shall I do about these Americans?'

'Send them back to Italy.'

The American Colonel was more than a little surprised when I gave him these instructions, but there was no time to argue, so I left him and drove off to Kifissia at top speed. The roads were choked with woodcutters and there were a lot of heavily armed ELAS on the roads. However, they didn't attempt to interfere with me. When I got there I found everyone at lunch — bully and biscuits — no fresh bread or meat has been on the ration ever since we got here, almost two months ago! That's what's called organization. The imperturbable Bob refused to talk business till we'd finished eating. Then we had our pow-wow! Short and sweet:

'Evacuate Tatoi. Get your whole Unit here by sundown. Move your men out of their billets into the HQ building and your officers into this Mess.'

Sundown. That gave me three hours. I phoned the Adjutant to get the thing started at Tatoi, then drove to the billet and told the senior Sergeant to start moving the men, then back to the airfield.

There were still miles of woodcutters, but the ELAS scouts had disappeared. It's no joke to move two hundred men, forty-two vehicles and about sixty tons of equipment over seven miles of narrow roads, half-blocked with woodcutters, in three hours! As I drove I was thinking hard: we should have to shuttle the three-tonners. Each vehicle must have a guard. We'd have to leave all the furniture and heavy wheel jacks. And the tents? We shouldn't be able to manage them in the time. An officer would have to be detailed to receive the stuff at Kifissia and park it all. The aircraft on the field would have to be sent to Hassani. And so on . . . Then there was the air traffic. That would go on. It was our job to deal with it and, if things got really sticky, it might be all-important, so a party would have to risk going through Athens to get there.

Of course at Tatoi we were miles from anywhere. Out on a limb. If trouble really developed, we could easily be cut off. There weren't any troops to spare to defend it. But still, I was damned angry at being run out of the place after all the work we'd put into it. As I wound through the deep ravines in the narrow road I kept thinking what a splendid place it would be for an ELAS ambush! But the place was free of all troops, only the damned woodcutters. They would slow up the three-tonners doing the shuttle.

At the field, pandemonium. Everyone working like mad. Richardson had already detailed his party for Hassani and we decided what vehicles to send with him and his essential equipment. I packed him off first, via Kifissia, so that the men could get their kit, told him to avoid the main streets in the centre of the city, gave him a Greek guide, one of our faithful men, and was glad to see him on his way. A prodigious afternoon's work followed, but by five thirty the whole place was cleared and all the stuff parked at Kifissia! It's wonderful what you can do when you try!

Later the AOC turned up from Athens. He had met Richardson with his whole convoy right in the centre of the town, standing in the middle of the road, calmly discussing with a Greek and a map the best road out to Hassani — with machine guns rattling away either side of him! But nothing worries Rich. He was last out of Cos, and this was child's play. I phoned Hassani and found he had arrived all right, no casualties. He was going to camp and work in a corner of the only hut that has part of the roof on. Good show.

Later I went round with the AOC while he harangued the men. They were all pretty mystified at the sudden change from peace to war conditions. Besides they were all rather jumpy and crowded together in the two HQ hotels, the so-called 'defended area'. He gave them a brief outline of the way the situation had deteriorated. How ELAS had claimed the right to run the Government and refused to lay down their arms, to arbitrate or negotiate, that attacks had been made on our men in the Piraeus, several had been killed, that the entire city had been paralysed and so General Scobie had reluctantly ordered a full offensive against ELAS. He emphasized we were not fighting the 'friendly' Greeks, but only the ELAS armed forces — less than 5% of the population. Minorities could not be allowed to seize power by force. The men listened attentively, but I felt they did not quite believe the gravity of the situation. They liked the Greeks and couldn't believe it would come to anything.

Air Attacks

But today the mood has changed. Everybody is a bit glum — no doubt a contrast to the rush of yesterday. We spent the time, in the beautiful sunshine, sorting kit and getting all the trucks serviceable. The men were depressed and their crowded living conditions were no help.

From the balcony of the hotel we could see the Spits and Beaufighters out, strafing targets in the city. Fighting is reported in the Piraeus and near the Acropolis. We have no idea how the situation is developing. but, as anyone can see, this place is no joke to defend. The two hotels in which we are billeted are about 100 yards apart. Around them stand villas, some of which still have 'friendly' Greek owners in them. There are a few Bofors guns, not dug in, commanding the roads, some machine guns on the roofs, two armoured cars, two companies of the RAF Regiment, but all the remaining six hundred men are RAF tradesmen. None of them are really trained to handle a gun and have no conception of field tactics or modern warfare.

The idea of bringing us all up here was that Kifissia is supposed to be defended by the Army. They have undertaken to back us up; but if things get tough, I don't see them sparing the men. We are eight miles out of the city. There is only one road, very open and vulnerable. If the road is cut, we are literally trapped, as I said. If things go against us, this is only a matter of time.

Convoys

I asked the AOC if I could send some men down to Hassani to reinforce the Traffic Section. He agreed. No sense in having the men up here, idle, when there is plenty of work down there. We spent all the morning loading up a convoy. Twenty vehicles with a guard of two armoured cars. I sent Flying Control, and some of the Servicing Section. They set off after lunch and I phoned later and heard they got through all right, only one man slightly wounded by machine-gun fire.

When the AOC got back tonight — he is all the time shuttling up and down to Athens in his armoured car — he said he thought I ought to get down to Hassani with as many men as he could take. He said that the position was worse, if anything, and that if it got desperate we should have to rely on air transport entirely. Already no ships could unload in the Piraeus. The Ops Squadrons are working full out and can't take care of any Transport Command problems.

I told him frankly I thought we were in a precarious situation. We had practically no water, little ammunition and not much food. If the road was cut and the Army couldn't spare us help, the place couldn't last long. We discussed it at some length and he instructed me to draw up a plan for evacuation. I don't think it can be done with the transport at our disposal under four days.

I came down from Kifissia on 8 December. We left at 0800 hours, a big convoy. All the Signals vehicles, enough men to man a Signal's watch, the cypher staff and some others. I was in the leading armoured car with the AOC. The long road was quite deserted and it wasn't until we got near Athens that bursts of machine-gun fire opened up from either side of the road. We pulled to one side and our gunner returned the fire, while the convoy speeded up and slipped past us, all okay. After that there was no further trouble and we reached Hassani un-molested.

Arrived there, I took one look at the waterlogged tents — it had been raining heavily during the night — and decided we must get the men under a roof forthwith. It was bitterly cold, there was no light and the cooks were in trouble with their stove. Still everyone was amazingly cheerful given the con-ditions.

The wooden huts were all lying about in heaps as they had been since the general strike started. Only a bit of a roof was up on one. Richardson had appropriated this and had impro-vised his section splendidly under the most primitive con-ditions. We all set to. By four o'clock we had the Signals chan-nels open and I rushed off and commandeered billets for our sixty men. I had already fixed up a Mess for ourselves a week or two before and we moved our own stuff down into that. As we closed down at dusk, a message came through that the road to Air HQ had been blocked and mined. Kifissia was cut off!

I thought it would come, but not so quickly. What will hap-pen to our chaps? The Army have too much on their plate to get up there and bring them out. It would take a hundred vehi-cles to move them and there aren't so many vehicles to spare. Our only link with them now is the Radio and the AOC's light aircraft, his little Auster. More for fun than anything else he had a strip cleared behind the hotel up at Kifissia. It is steep as the side of a house. You land uphill and take off downhill — whatever the wind! All day yesterday and today he has been ferrying to and fro in the little machine bringing out key personnel and taking in mail and urgent supplies.

Curious that, however technical a unit, it succeeds or fails, not by lapses of skill (which are rare) but by good or bad administration, discipline and food. If you've got a good cook you've got a good unit. If you've got a good cook and good housekeeper, i.e. a good adjutant, you're home and dry. In this technical age there isn't much difficulty with functional efficiency, the headaches are always domestic. So when the AOC said he could fly me out three men, I chose, not wireless operators or fitters, but my Orderly Room Corporal and two cooks.

Guerrilla War

How circumstances alter what you see in things! As I stood yesterday evening among the piles of timber waiting to be made into huts and looked out over the Gulf of Athens, I could see before me the emptiness of the airfield and the runway slightly tilted towards the water.

Beyond, the sea, sparkling in the evening light, seemed incredibly lucid and glistening. Out in the bay the island of Aegina was a block of pure lapis. To the right Salamis, owing to some refractive effect I have never seen before, was levitated clear of the water! An aerial island! Further to the right was the hump of the Piraeus, thickly built up and from there the eye ran inland to Athens itself, poured white over its sacred hills. Behind me the ground swooped swiftly upwards to the slopes of Mount Hymettus, washed with violet.

It is, I suppose, as fine a prospect as any in the world, but I wasn't thinking of beauty just then, I was watching the arc of red sparks that sailed up leisurely from some point out in the bay and was lost in the Piraeus hillside. 'Pom-poms,' I said to myself, 'from an offshore MTB.' Several other arcs appeared as more guns opened up, then one in which the sparks curved seaward. 'That means ELAS hold the high ground overlooking the Piraeus,' I reflected. I looked up to Hymettus behind me. A battery of guns up there would command the whole airfield. They could smash the runways and the parked aircraft. Even a few well-placed machine guns could do a lot of damage. One hole through an undercart or a tank would put an aircraft out of action.

As I drove down to our Mess, a villa on the sea's edge, I was thinking, not of its superb position, but of where to site guards and strong points. I stopped at the men's billets and wondered how defensible I could make them in an emergency, of the direction from which any attack was likely to develop. Greeks, from their doorways, staring at me as I passed, all turned into spies following where I went. The whole place grew eyes and a feeling of being watched.

The devil of it is there is no 'front'. The front might be the side or the back! Any wall could conceal a mortar, any window a machine gun. The men who fired them could loose off a few shots, kill a few of our chaps, then stick their weapons up the chimney and walk out of the front door as 'friendly' Geeks! We are not fighting friendly Greeks. But who are they? In this sort of situation, heavily outnumbered as we are, with small units scattered all over Athens and the Piraeus, it's all just about as tricky as any military situation could be.

Help! [*]

10 December.

Great news! The Fourth Division, on its way from Italy to 'rest' in Palestine, is being diverted here. Major-General Dudley Ward

---

[*]Obviously, no factual details of these operations were included in my letters written home at this time.

and staff arrived by air, shortly followed by Field-Marshal Alexander. The situation in the city is so serious that even Alex has to wait three hours before an armoured vehicle can be spared to get him up to HQ. Dudley Ward has to wait (in our Mess) until ten at night! Then a Colonel, wounded coming down in his jeep, arrived to escort him in. The Colonel takes a gloomy view of the situation, on which he talks very well. Heavy firing over Athens all night.

11 December

I suppose the situation must have been more critical than any of us had realized. Evidently Alex sent a high-powered signal, for today, at midday, the rush started. Eighty-one aircraft, Libs and Dakotas, were signalled. That meant nearly three hundred tons of men and equipment! We have about twelve vehicles and couldn't possibly cope with the unloading. Then Dudley Ward turned up.

'Want any help, Lewis?' he enquired.

'Fifty trucks and a hundred bodies,' I told him.

An hour later he produced them.

Meanwhile we hurriedly improvised a plan. It seemed essential, if we were to deal successfully with large numbers of aircraft in a short space of time, to park them so that they could be quickly turned round for take off and return to base. If we got into congestion and delay the aircraft wouldn't get away to Italy that night, ready to bring in more stuff tomorrow. Quite apart from that, we couldn't possibly sleep the crews!

F/Lt Stockall, my Flying Control Officer, an ex-Canadian schoolmaster, was in his element. Slow and imperturbable, he made a recce of the field and came back with his plan, scrawled on the back of an envelope and drawled that he 'guessed' we could handle it. Meanwhile the cooks were turned on to brew up tea, bully and biscuits for three hundred aircrew. The lorries, as they turned up, were parked strategically in a line, with an unloading crew to each. All our men who could be spared joined the army bods. An Army Officer supervised the 'rank' of trucks. It was quite an impressive set-up when the whole lot was ready to receive aircraft — and that was about ten minutes before they were due to arrive!

Suddenly the air seemed thick with aircraft!

The whole eighty arrived within the hour!

It was a really magnificent demonstration of air power and pilot skill. One of the few examples, I imagine, of how vital forces delivered quickly in a critical situation can change the whole course of events. The big Libs swept down hard on each other's tails one after another, their deep bellies almost touching the ground, swayed a bit, wheeled off the runway just in time to clear the one following. Our jeep piloted them up to the park. A truck peeled off the rank. Before the props had stopped it had backed up to the aircraft and the unloading crew swarmed in to get hold of the stuff.

Soon the whole field was covered with aircraft. Trucks rushed to the dumps, unloaded and came back for more. Two battalions of troops aboard the Daks were assembled at marshalling points with their kits. The aircrew got their tea and within three hours the whole armada, eighty-one aircraft, had started up, got in line for take off and wheeled away towards the Gulf of Corinth and Italy!

By dusk all the ammo had been carted off to the dumps and the airfield was as quiet and deserted as it has been in the morning. Geoffrey Tuttle sent us a note of congratulation on the way the job had been handled and I stuck this up in the men's Mess for all to see. Some of the troops that arrived have been detailed to guard the airfield. As it is our only link with the outside world, this seems an admirable idea — or at least we think so!

12 December

Our biggest day! We received one hundred and thirteen aircraft; Liberators, Wellingtons and Dakotas. Again there was no spacing and the whole lot arrived around lunchtime. The air was absolutely thick with kites trying to get in and trying to get out. It was nothing to see twelve Libs on 'finals' at the same time, dropping their wheels, stepped up one behind the other in a long line down on to the runway.

When it got too hot, the AC 'plonk', the boy on the end of the runway, who had the job of trying to space them out and get a decent interval between landings, fired a 'red'. But many of the cartridges were faulty, the red didn't go off and, by the time he had reloaded, the whole situation had changed! One crash on the runway would have put the whole operation out of action, for we had no gear powerful enough to drag such heavy machines clear. However, our luck held and, although there were some near shaves, the whole lot got down without mishap.

It was a pretty inspiring exhibition of air power to see this great convoy arrive, but I was too busy to admire it for the unloading was a headache and, for a time, the thing seemed to get out of hand. But, well before dusk we got all the loads off and away to the dumps.

It must be remembered that, besides all these 'transport' aircraft, there were squadrons of Spits, Beaufighters and Wellingtons, all operating vital 'offensive' operations off this one runway! Often twenty aircraft were lined up waiting to take off, while streams of others had the priority, coming in.

There was something electrical in the atmosphere. I think everyone realized it was one of those big moments when everything came together: the air attacks on the Piraeus, the arrival of men and materials by air, the start of the house-to-house fight for the city. The heart of the whole operation was here, on the airfield. If ELAS had managed to get one gun into action on Hymettus, there, above us — and there was nothing whatever to stop them — the whole course of events would have been different. But they didn't. The airfield was never attacked.

Then the weather clamped! Only sixty aircraft managed to get away. That left us with about two hundred and fifty aircrew to feed and sleep! We managed the evening meal, but the boys had to sleep in their machines. It was bloody cold, but they didn't grumble — though some did enquire about the odds of being shot up during the night! We reassured them, but of course we were in a bit of a spot. ELAS seem to control all the Piraeus. They have the British Embassy under fire. The Corps HQ building, right in the centre of Athens, is being pooped at by a 75 all day. It doesn't seem to be doing much damage, but the boys don't seem to like it. Can't think why! General Hawksworth, who everyone says is first class, is coming in to fight the city battle. We are preparing beachheads near the airfield. One cannot complain that life is dull.

14 December

The weather remained n.b.g. all next day and we hardly got an aircraft in. We were glad of the rest. It made it possible for us to get away all those that had been stuck here for the night. Our regular daily schedule from Italy has been withdrawn. They must be pretty windy back there. Hassani, for the moment, is perfectly safe but the cancellation means we get nothing in, particularly mail, which is more important than ever just now.

We all got together and had a natter about the job. Half the frantic rush would be avoided if we could get incoming convoys spaced out at hour intervals. We could unload with less trucks and men and the whole operation would be very much simplified. Signalled Italy to this effect.

Our chippy, with a couple of men to help him, is tackling the job of getting some more roofs on the huts. He is doing well, but the walls don't fit and the icy winds come whistling through everywhere. We stamp about in our overcoats, trying to work and keep warm. Standing in line for our bully and biscuits is a freezing way to eat, but there's no option. We aren't inclined to dawdle over the luncheon break, that's one thing: but we're organizing a hot meal in dixies for tomorrow.

Not much news of the battle, but we hear they have managed to clear a bit of the dock area, enough to get the rest of the 4th

Division in by sea. If we can hold it for the next few days the position should improve.

15 December

The last of the aircraft from the 13th get away. We received sixty others, Liberators and Dakotas; but our signal has taken effect, the aircraft are better spaced and everybody now knows the job and the whole thing goes with a swing. Three cineprojectors arrive from Cairo. We took one, one went to Wing and the other was flown into Kifissia by Geoffrey with a Sergeant to operate it.

The situation there is damnable. The chaps are marooned and if ELAS make a determined attack, before we can get them reinforcements, I don't see how we can hold it. It bothers me because, apart from anything else, we can't go on running this show with only sixty bods and ten officers, of whom three are quite new to the work.

Then there is Salonika. I have twenty men and an officer there. The situation is said to be tense, with ELAS in complete control. It may boil up at any moment. I feel I must get my chaps out of it. There's no traffic to justify them staying up there and an extra twenty bods would make a lot of difference in coping with the rush down here.

An Army type comes in from Patras. He tells me the same story. ELAS in complete control, getting daily more menacing, while he hadn't enough men or food. No help can possibly be got out to Patras at the moment. We may be in difficulties here, but at least we are in touch with the outside world. I feel sorry for the chaps who are really cut off.

16 December

Last night the HQ of the 23rd Armoured Brigade was attacked, right in the centre of Athens, near the Embassy. ELAS dynamited a hole in the wall of the compound, shot three officers in their beds and fired some vehicles. Our chaps fought them back and by morning had regained almost the whole area.

This was a daring attack, carefully planned and well carried out. ELAS of course realize that all our communications depend on the tanks and armoured cars of the Brigade. If they managed to put them out, it would be a most serious setback. No thin-skinned vehicles can operate over most of Athens. There seems to be a definite plan to draw a circle round Corps HQ and eliminate it. The shelling of the building continues. Nobody has yet been able to spot the site of the gun which must be placed in a house overlooking the building, somewhere in the town.

Today only forty aircraft arrived. Money for jam! 178 Squadron, the Libs, have made the Staging Post a gift of a whole case of cigarettes and chocolate! Enough for 50 cigarettes a man! They all ante-ed up and apparently threw their ration into a box which their Group Captain flew over. Damn decent! Most people wouldn't bother with another Unit like that. I wrote to their CO from all of us, thanking him, and stuck a copy of the letter up in the men's Mess so they would know it had been done.

17 December

Half-way down the Leoforos Syngrou, the main artery from the coast to Athens, stands a big brewery. It is an ELAS strongpoint. They fire from the roof at every vehicle going up and down the road. This morning two 3-tonners were allowed to come down bringing passengers to the airfield. 'Normal risks of war'. One passenger, a Sergeant, going home, after completing his term of service overseas. was shot through the head. The others were wounded. I was furious about this. If the road isn't safe, it mustn't be used by thin-skinned vehicles. In future passengers will come out to the field the previous night and sleep here. They'll be damned uncomfortable — but alive. And that's the main thing.

The rocket Beaufighters have arrived! At last! Now we ought

to make some progress. There are signs that Hawksworth is getting under way. At least the airfield is well defended. Up to two days ago it could easily have been overrun and then we should have been back to the beaches. It's been touch and go.

18 December

Kifissia has been attacked! The Beaus and Spits are out, strafing. We hear that one of our chaps has been shot whilst on guard. We hear they are short of ammo. A Halifax is rushed in to drop supplies, but the area is difficult for a stranger to pinpoint. He misses and they don't get the stuff. ELAS do. Damnation.

We receive sixty aircraft and evacuate UNRA personnel. The airfield at Salonika is unserviceable — rain. With this attack on Kifissia and the general situation, I am getting more worried still about our chaps up north. We mut get them out. No news of how the attack on Kifissia is going. But an armoured car column has been sent up to relieve them.

19 December

At 1100 hours I received orders to hold five Dakotas. Some of our chaps from Kifissia were said to have got out and were making for Tatoi where we could nip over and pick them up. An hour of suspense. Then the AOC drove up and told me that Air HQ had fallen. A column of prisoners had been seen moving up the road from Kifissia to Tatoi. It was hoped to scare away their guards with Spits and get them to Tatoi. Another hour of suspense. Then word came through that the operation was not practical and was to be abandoned. We all wonder how many of our poor chaps have gone. It is bitterly cold, snow on the mountains, a biting wind and they are marching North into that.

The Salonika detachment gets in! Thank heaven for that, anyway! We handle sixty-eight aircraft.

20 December

We hear that the relief battalion got to Kifissia only an hour after the place had fallen. Twenty of my chaps have got out! They were on guard and retreated to the Hotel Olympus, where they hid on an upper floor. They kept perfectly still, watching the looting and firing of everything. When the tanks arrived and the ELAS scattered, they ran down, got on the tanks, started up four of our vehicles and drove them down here under escort. They were all a bit shaken, but otherwise okay. Good show!

Macmillan leaves for Marcianise to see Alexander. I talk to him while he waits for his aircraft. He has been up in Athens through all this trying to negotiate with the Greeks, but makes no progress. They double-cross him all the time. He tells me of his idea to set up a Regency under Archbishop Damaskinos. Brilliant! Apparently everybody agrees with this, except the King — back in Claridges! What a situation!

It is a very cold, very busy day. We handle eighty-three aircraft! The general situation is improving. The coup, as such, has failed, but there is still plenty of fighting. Guns going all day and night. The Beaus have pranged ELAS HQ. Twelve rockets. Finish.

21 December

It is alleged that Hassani is under gunfire, though I never saw anything myself! Anyhow we disperse aircraft more widely and arrange another system of marshalling. W/Cmdr Francombe, the CO of the Dakotas at Bari, flies us in fresh bread and sweets. Stubbs sends us up soap and tea from the Delta.

Scobie's announcement that he will open fire on every ELAS position with everything he's got and his advice to the civilian population to make themselves scarce has resulted in a horde of Greeks migrating out to us — 'for protection'. But I've heard that before! They infiltrated Kifissia in the same way. Then the houses within the perimeter sprouted machine guns. I did a search in my own billet last night and found ammo in the basement. The devil of it is you never know where the next shots will come from. I am having a guard put on my billet.

Aircraft are out trying to spot the prisoners. They report snow on the mountains. It is cold enough here at sea level and our hearts go out to our poor chaps in ELAS hands. No sign of them today.

Every account of an engagement must vary with the person who makes it, so my talk with the boys who got out of Kifissia didn't give much idea of the general engagement. It appears that the first attack was launched on our Air HQ at the Cecil Hotel. Guns and mortars opened up from the gully where the hotel stood. The first salvo knocked out the War Room, the second the Radio transmitter and the third the cookhouse. Simultaneously the other hotel, the Pentelikon, was attacked. Then the two hotels, which stood some two hundred yards apart, were soon cut off from each other and my chaps who were on guard round the Cecil don't quite know when it fell. It appears they blew a hole in the wall and swarmed in through the gap, over-running the place before anybody could put up any effective defence.

They seemed to know the disposition of our defence points quite accurately. This is not surprising because all day long before the attack Greeks were allowed to wander about in our 'defended' area. Nobody bothered them. They were 'friendly' Greeks. Some of our own Greeks pointed them out to us but nobody paid much attention. No attempt was made to clear the defended area of all civilians; that would have involved turning friendly Greeks out of their homes!

However, the action seems to have gone on most of the 18th until our ammunition was exhausted. Then a determined attack was made on the hotel. They got into the passages with a machine gun and then there wasn't much we could do about it.

Finally, when grenades were thrown on our wounded in the basement, our people threw in their hands. Girls of fifteen and sixteen were in the first assault and it is said that about a thousand ELAS troops were engaged. But they were followed by a disorganized rabble just out to loot. The 'regular' ELAS troops rounded up our prisoners and marched them out of the village without delay, leaving the rest to pillage.

22 December

Adjutant, and I try to take stock of the situation. We have lost seventy-five officers and men, thirty-eight vehicles and the bulk of our equipment. The entire Orderly Room records are lost. All the men's personal documents, all the Personnel occurrence reports, all the pay increments and release group records (which had taken weeks to work out). In addition we have lost our aircraft refuellers, our water bowsers, our three-tonners, 15-cwts, jeeps, all our night flying flare path equipment, our servicing flight spares and stores — everything. It will mean practically starting the unit from scratch.

Bad enough when there's no aircraft flow: but now, with all the stuff coming in, it's going to be a headache. I'm sorry for my Adjutant, Blom Peachey, seeing him carrying on quite cheerfully in the middle of all this, with only one clerk to help him. He's a splendid officer.

We managed to get some clothes for our chaps that got out of Kifissia; they have lost all of everything, of course.

Interesting to watch how the Americans have behaved through all this. Greece has been agreed an all-British sphere of operations; but within forty-eight hours of our arrival, a Mission from their HQ turned up to select an airfield (of which they demanded exclusive use) to set up their show. It was toally unnecessary, of course, but America is playing for post-war stakes. She wants to get her foot in here. It is an indispensible link in running services to the Far East. Ultimately she set up at Eleusis with three hundred men and thirty officers, all with nothing to do — for the present.

When this 'war' started up, their Officer-in-Charge went to ELAS and pointed out they were a strictly non-combat unit, carrying only American personnel. So ELAS allowed them to carry on, unmolested. They just cover their vehicles with American flags and move around as if nothing at all was the matter. To them it's all a joke. 'We're strictly neutral in this war!' they say, and, as usual, we carry the can.

To top it off they put on a posh luncheon party for all the big wigs, Greek Church and state, army and airforce with invites to us, of course. I didn't go. I was told there was so much food, huge steaks, lavish sweets and unlimited booze, of course, it was disgusting. I suppose they thought it was a show of American hospitality, but all our people have been living off emergency rations since we came in, so, as far as we were concerned, it was more of an insult than anything else.

23 December

It blew a bitter northern gale. Only three aircraft in all day. The chippies working away stubbornly on the huts. I think we shall get another one finished by the New Year. Dirty and draughty, but it will have to do.

The war continues but there is a marked increase now in the weight of artillery fire which booms away day and night. They are getting Athens clear — slowly. The road to town isn't safe yet. They're mounting an attack to take the brewery. We hear that's coming off shortly. In Piraeus it's still very tough. Yesterday an all-day engagement for the railway station there. We got it, but at quite a price. But the toughest fighting, they say, is round Ommonia Square, right in the centre of Athens. Apparently it's pretty badly knocked about.

24 December

The gale continues. Nothing in from Italy. But Stubbs, back in Cairo, sends us up 500 lbs of Welfare stuff. We shall be able to make a bit of a show for the men's Xmas dinner, after all.

Christmas Day

There was a flap on most of the day owing to Winston's sudden arrival. I must say, to leave his own fireside and come right across Europe to settle, or try to settle this business, shows a selflessness and statesmanlikeness in keeping with the great spirit he has shown us throughout the war.

I gather the Press have given a highly distorted view of the whole situation and it will certainly be good to have it set straight. During the morning Alex turned up with Eden. Macmillan later. At three the Prime's big silver Skymaster hove in sight. We had tanks, guards and escorts on the field. The gale still blew bitterly from the North.

Churchill appeared at the door of his aircraft for a moment, dressed in an Air Commodore's uniform, but he evidently didn't like the temperature, for he retired hurriedly. Then the others joined him for a preliminary conference.

This kept the rest of us stamping about in the freezing gale for the next two hours. Then the party moved off in armoured vehicles to the cruiser *Ajax*, which is lying off the Piraeus. We undertook to entertain Churchill's aircrew. They had had the foresight to bring along a barrel of beer with them, which they carefully prized out of the belly of the aircraft. We took them down to our Mess, where they will have to sleep in armchairs. Not much of an Xmas for them.

Then I rushed off with my officers to serve the men's Xmas dinner, our traditional custom. They had soup, tinned turkey, fresh vegetables, Christmas Pudding, oranges and nuts. I think they were surprised and pleased, knowing how difficult it had been to get anything. During the meal, one of the boys played carols on the piano and, as we officers rushed about serving the men, they all sang the old tunes. Then the lights went out, but the men continued singing by lantern-light.

There were little Xmas trees on the long tables and the dim light, the cigarettes, the voices singing those hymns that perhaps more than anything else take men back home, to their loved ones, so far away on this day, moved me a good deal. We have come through a tight spot together. Half our chaps are out somewhere in those freezing mountains. When I spoke to them afterwards and told them that two hundred had been located by the Swedish Red Cross in a Monastery some thirty miles north of Athens, a cheer went up I shall never forget.

After that we went back to our own dinner. Ivor had managed to come down and spend Xmas with me. He got here a few days ago and we shot him off down to Cairo where he shopped for the Mess to great effect, coming back laden with good things, so we had a real spread and settled down to deal with the barrel of beer. A public announcement was made on the radio that a Conference between all the parties has been called by Churchill for tomorrow. Well, if Churchill, Eden, Alexander and Macmillan can't solve it, nobody can.

26 December

I went to bed early, but was wakened about eleven by one of my officers coming to the billet to tell me that the airfield was under attack! I dressed quickly and went over to the Mess to find that something of a flap was on. Our huts in the centre of the field were said to have been under machine-gun fire.

The Duty Officer had put the night staff into a 15-cwt, together with all our secret and confidential documents, codes, cyphers, etc and brought them all down to the Mess. But the Cypher Officer and one Wireless Operator had been left behind. Why? It all sounded like a bit of a panic; but obviulsy two of our chaps couldn't be abandoned on the field like that. Also our transmitter had apparently gone off the air without giving a closing down signal — and I knew that would start a flap all over the Med. So it was necessary to investigate.

As I climbed into the jeep, Stockall appeared with a Sten gun and swung in beside me. 'I'll come with you, Sir.' he said quietly. With another jeep and gunner as escort, we set out. We were frequently challenged, but when we got to the field — it was something of an anticlimax — everything was dead quiet! We found the two chaps, safe and sound. There had been quite a bit of firing, they said, but it had all fizzled out.

Later we found out that six machine guns were said to have opened up on the field from the hills at extreme range. An ELAS 'soldier' had come in, given himself up, and told us an attack would develop in half an hour. Of course nobody believed him and while they were trying to sort this out, sure enough the firing began! The thing began to look farcical.

We rushed down to make sure that Winston's aircraft was okay to find the Steward fast asleep in bed, having heard nothing! On the way there, we were shot at by a Greek sentry, very trigger happy. He missed us comfortably! The Admin Channel of the R/T was re-opened and we waited in the Mess for the All Clear. This came at 1.30 in the morning. The boys all went back to their posts and the rest of the night was quiet.

But next morning General Hawksworth appeared. I was very surprised. Why, he enquired, had I withdrawn my men from the field and 'retreated' before an attack had even developed? I told him that I had given orders that, in the event of attack, all cyphers and secret documents were to be withdrawn from the field at once; but the personnel were to remain. This is what had been done. But he still was not satisfied and wanted to know why the two clerks had come down with the cyphers. 'Because they were responsible for their cyphers and documents.' He seemed only half-satisfied and left.

He left me with a very sharp impression of what it means to fight a battle. First that he was on to a small incident like this right away, second that his attitude to everything was attack. He would not tolerate anything less. I decided to look at all my orders — which I knew had been inadequate — only to be given the Defence of the Airfield Orders document — which had just that moment arrived! They had forgotten to put me on the distribution list! Typical!

This started me doing all the things I ought to have done days earlier, digging trenches, sandbagging vehicles, etc, etc. At 5.30 pm I paraded all the men and gave them instructions as to rotas for guarding our six billets and messes, besides the huts and aircraft on the field and generally getting the whole thing clued up. I felt easier in my mind when all this had been done, though we have plenty of forces here round Hassani and I don't think there's much chance of any attack.

27 December

The plot to blow up the Grande Bretagne Hotel and the 3rd Corps HQ by placing charges in the main sewer that runs under the buildings created quite a stir. More by luck than anything else it was discovered just in time.

The Conference called by Churchill doesn't seem to have made much progress. True, they have accepted the idea of a Regent, but their demands for representation on the government are so exhorbitant that they are unacceptable to other parties and to us.

Fighting continues. Rumours of a big general advance being mounted today. But when we have cleared Athens and the Piraeus how much nearer are we to peace in Greece? Macmillan said he saw no solution either military or political. But there's always the chance that they may get tired of it or it may fizzle out.

Churchill leaves. We all gathered to cheer him and he came and spoke to us for a moment before going on board. His aircraft is the last word in luxury and surprised us all by its short take off and rapid climb.

I am sitting propped up in bed, writing this. Only eight o'clock but, owing to the shortage of fuel — a perambulator of wood costs £14 — and the strict rationing of paraffin and coal, bed is the warmest place! Jumper, dressing gown, socks and six blankets make me almost comfortable! The weather is dreadfully cold; northerly gales and stone floors, draughty doors and windows are not a good combination.

I am interested to hear that 'everyone' at home sympathizes with the rebels. I wish they could come here and see for themselves. The whole thing has been grossly misrepresented in the world press and perhaps that is our fault for not taking it seriously enough. Our propaganda is always a bit slow getting under way. However, whatever people at home think, I, for one, have not given ten years of my life defending the democratic principle to be content to see the first 'liberated' country in Europe fall victim to an opportunist communistic minority, trying to shoot its way to power with a few Tommy guns. This is exactly the sort of terrorism by which Hitler gained power. If people at home sympathize with this, well, all I can say is they are pretty poor democrats. But I prefer to blame the press. I met some of them when they came out. They had a very cheap and shoddy point of view. They seemed to want to fault us. Anything for a showy headline!

However, I would be glad if the suggestion of an international force sent in to maintain peace and order were put into effect. I really see no reason why we should carry the odium of these local squabbles. Everybody here knows already that Greeks can never agree about anything, never do anything together, talk their heads off and end up with nothing.

And all this stuttering of machine guns and thudding of mortars is taking place in days of the most perfect crystalline beauty I have ever seen! It is as if our eyes and our ears lived in two different worlds. . .

Tomorrow is New Year's Eve. I shall have been away from

you for over a year! It seems longer. Overseas these festive dates
are really depressing. Everybody wants to be near those they
love and the forced gaiety seems to increase the emptiness. We
have been through quite a tough spot. While it was on we
hadn't much time to think, but now it is over, more or less,
we are suffering the anticlimax. Inside I can find no rest, but
outwardly, of course, I put up some sort of show, since, in the
unit, everything revolves round me and all come expecting
answers, or at least sympathy, understanding and interest in all
their troubles and cares. On the whole I manage to cope, but
oh, if I could be alone for a bit and sit and put my feet up —
with you.

12 January

Now the truce has been signed, everything shows signs of
reverting to normal. We have at least reached the stage our
Greek staff call 'finito Boum, Boum!'

The first of our chaps taken prisoner has managed to get back.
His hair is almost white. It seems to have been pretty rough.
When things began to go badly for ELAS some of them wanted
to shoot all the prisoners out of hand, while others began to fra-
ternize with them. He finished up in a secret hideout in the basement of a house where his captor, now quite demoralized, begged to be taken prisoner. What a situation!

This mob of thugs and bandits, towards whom everyone at
home seems so friendly, thinks of nothing but loot and booty.
They robbed our chaps of everything, watches, rings, mufflers,
boots. I suppose some think such things legitimate but I would
like people to see the vandalism they have left in their train.

I revisited our billets at Tatoi. I have never seen anything like
it. Not a stick left. Everything had been looted, furniture, doors,
window frames, even floors, ripped out, destroyed, smashed for
firewood. At the airfield I couldn't believe my eyes. Absolutely
useless things had gone, huge scrapped aero engines, weighing
hundreds of pounds, technical gear of which they can't even

have known the use, a huge amount of stuff which must have needed hundreds of carts or lorries to move — all, bar our domestic stuff, quite, quite useless.

Somehow this was more terrible than the inhuman destruction of bombing. It was the barbarism of men gone mad with greed and nihilism and it left a very ugly taste in my mouth — as if one had suddenly been allowed to see into the black depths of men's souls. How terribly thin is the veneer of our so-called civilization. How much evil still seems to grow in the world. How men seem to have a genius to turn good to bad. How much easier it is to destroy than create.

As I looked on all this I really felt our civilization was doomed, doomed to immolate itself, on the altar of its own greed and imbecility. We have eaten some deadly virus, like Sanderson fed to those parasol ants which made them mad to fight each other, the poison spreading with each bite until the whole colony immolated itself in an orgy of self-destruction.

Then suddenly this evening, after a stormy day, the sun burst through banks of cloud between the islands and the sea. A violent glow suffused the air and washed all the mountains gold; all the houses, the sea, the barren trees were bathed in this sudden glory of light. It only lasted a few moments. Then the darkness came back and the stars looked brittle in the wind.

Prisoners' Return

Yesterday all the men taken prisoners by ELAS at Kifissia came back. I spent most of the day with them. A few are in hospital temporarily, but the rest are fit, though the strain of the experience shows in all their faces. Some look much older. They were marched 160 miles in under a fortnight, mostly without shoes or overcoats, through snow-covered passes, sleeping on bare stone floors without covering or fire. They had very little food; black bread and a handful of figs made their meals until our supply-dropping got organized.

The morale remained very high throughout and deeds of kindness and strength of character abound on all sides. We are a wonderful people in adversity. Heaven knows how long they would have gone on, but most of them say the moment they set foot on the gangplank of the steamer that brought them back from the north was the most wonderful moment of their lives. Their feet were blistered and raw. Many suffered from frostbite. Some had the most extraordinary escapes, such as turning turtle in a truck and falling twelve feet over the road's edge into a gully and all coming out with nothing more than bruises. Throughout, the greatest disorganization prevailed among ELAS. Orders, counter-orders, all without purpose or aim. They all seem quieter for it. I fancy they will remember it all their lives.

I find it has all upset me deeply. I feel somehow as though I ought to have prevented it, foreseen it. I have all sorts of fantasies of guilt, regret, because I happened to get out and they didn't. I feel I ought to have been through it with them.

Of course the whole thing has had a striking effect on all of us in our feelings for the Greeks. When we arrived I remember thinking they were true allies, true friends and I was filled with warmth and admiration towards them for their suffering and loyalty. Now, you will not find a man who has a good word to say for them.

I am not a vindictive man, not a good hater. When I don't like people, I simply keep out of their way; but here, of course, I can't. I have to deal with Greeks all the time. I find I have a sort of blank inside. I don't believe anybody, trust anybody — even those who have stuck to us — and, because I am sanguine by nature, I find it all dreadfully depressing. Never mind. I expect it will pass.

The Greeks feel much the same about the Italians. The way they strutted about as conquerors here, when the Greeks have always beaten them, makes them livid. But of course all Greeks have a lively sense of humour, of the absurd. So, one day, during the occupation, when a Bersaglieri sat down at a cafe for a drink, putting his hat with its huge bunch of cock feathers on the seat beside him, he found when he picked it up it had laid two hen's eggs!

The Bay Of Salamis

Today was the best I have spent in Greece, the first day I have felt, since the truce was signed, that we are really at peace. I set off with one of my officers to inspect the little cruiser I have chartered for the summer. She is being cleaned and painted up for me by the Navy at one of the yards in the Bay of Salamis. We found her, *Aphrodite*, an old English south coast hull, encrusted with barnacles, but with her copper sheathing intact. I suppose she was built about fifty years ago, beamy, good oak timbers, just the job to potter about the islands — if I ever have time.

We walked on along the coast. Across the bay, only a mile or so away, lay the island of Salamis and it seemed impossible that one of the most famous naval battles of history should have been fought in this narrow stretch of water not wide enough to manoeuvre a destroyer in.

As we came over the rise we saw before us a whole colony of shipyards. They stretched along the coast for half a mile or more. We could hear the tapping of mallets and the sound of saws.

It was a lively scene, blue water, gaunt hills running up from the shore and this vista of hulls, masts and shrouds. I suppose there must have been fifty to a hundred caiques building, all in the open. Caiques of all sizes, some not much bigger than row-boats, some weighing hundreds of tons, bigger than Wallis' *Dolphin,* bigger than Columbus' *Santa Maria.*

As we got in among them, we found the whole place a bustle of activity. They say Greece is broke and everything is at a standstill, but there didn't seem any sign of it here. And a good thing too. There can't be anything more urgent than to get the island trade going. There were old caiques, black with pitch and age, being patched and caulked and scraped, there were new caiques just being planked, fresh in their first coats of red lead — which in this light turns them to a delicate shade of rose. There were great skeletons of frames, soaring stems and rudder posts, bleached pale gold against the sky — the time when a building boat looks most romantic, I think.

Everywhere was the sound of shipwrights at work, driving spikes, swinging long-handled adzes or using slim two-handled saws. There were boats being built under the shade of trees, boats with goats asleep underneath them, boats poking their prows over the walls of gardens so that I couldn't see how they could be got out without breaking the walls, boats lifting delicate sheers between the trunks of pine trees, nosing out of the green towards the blue, boats painted peagreen or vermilion, with carved coamings and new masts, boats, boats, boats as far as the eye could see.

Work was going on everywhere. Boys, hardly old enough to hold a maul, were driving spikes under the turn of the bilges of one old hulk, old men were expertly eyeing timber for another, women were spinning out caulking wool between their fingers, sitting in the sun, others were laying piles of dry grass and scrub under the dirty bilges of an old hull to which they set fire. The stubble soon burnt out, leaving the hull clean of its barnacles. One old man, who must have been the patriarch of all boat-builders, a veritable Noah, in a black velvet skull cap, tight-fitting black coat and enormous blue plus-fours, relic of god knows what Turkish ancestry, was sitting blinking in the sun and only woke when he saw my camera.

We clambered up a big ladder on to the deck of the largest wooden ship I have ever seen. She must have been of four hundred tons burden. She stood a good thirty feet above the ways and had a magnificent bold sheer. When you stood aft, the deck curled up like the tongue of a panting dog. This great ship hadn't had a drop of paint. She was pale gold all over. She must have been standing in the sun for many years. By the sternpost was a huge cast brass three-bladed propellor, lying polished in the sun.

I suppose there aren't many places left where the making of wooden ships is still a living trade. They told me seamen can tell at a glance from the line of her sheer the island where a caique was built.

I came away quite rested and refreshed. Something was being created here. An old craft was still alive and flourishing. It brought a feeling of hope and peace. Returning through the demolished streets and squalor of the Piraeus I could still see that golden hull against the sky and smell the scents of fresh paint and cut wood.

The Parthenon

I started off the day by helping a shepherd girl to capture two kids. They were gambolling and frisking around outside my window in that enchanting lollipop way they have. By a combined effort we managed to catch one, which I nursed while she went after the other. Mine was brown and white with flop ears and called continuously to its brother. I held it under its tummy and its too-big feet dangled adorably. It smelt so fresh and clean.

The other one got mixed up with some sheep, but finally the little barefoot shepherdess managed to capture that too. He was black and white and equally adorable. So I handed mine over to the child, who tucked one under each arm and started to drive the flock away. But immediately they took the wrong turning and, without a second's hesitation, she dropped the kids and started after the sheep! Heigho! So all's to do again, I thought, and left her to it. Still, it was a nice way to start the day.

All these months going up and down to Athens I have seen the Parthenon standing serene on the Acropolis and put off going to look at it, partly because I was too busy and partly because I wanted to be in the right mood. But yesterday, coming back from a party at a taverna outside the town — it was full moon

— somebody suggested 'Would you like to see the Parthenon? Let's go up. It's only open at full moon.' It seemed the right moment, so up we went.

The night was full of misty moonlight, thick as a September moon in England. Everything was veiled, yet it was bright enough to read by. As we climbed the broken-down steps, above us lay a grove of silver pillars. They were like the first notes of an overture by which the listener is gripped and led on to all that follows. For the next half hour I was really in a sort of trance so great and unexpected was the experience upon me. I had a sense of profound felicity and peace. D. H. Lawrence says somewhere that certain spots are spiritual nerve centres, places where, for no reason we can define, men and women, receptive to such things, find themselves overcome with something, which for want of a better phrase, we call the spirit of God. The Acropolis is without doubt such a place and it is impossible to describe the feeling.

At the head of the steps, set out on a corner of rock, so that a casual visitor might easily pass it by, stands the tiny Temple of Wingless Victory. I saw it bathed in moonlight and framed between two enormous pillars. It hit me like a blow, I couldn't speak. I had actual difficulty in getting my breath. They were pointing to this and that, inviting me to look here and there, but something had happened. I suppose I must have replied, but I remember absolutely nothing.

We wandered on through aisles of striped moonlight in the shades of the Parthenon, looked down on the blue Athenian night and up through vistas of cream shafts that seemed to climb beyond the dreams of men. Somehow or other we left it all and came away. I don't ever want to spoil it by going back.

If only . . .

What a strange experience Greece has been for me! Waves of wonder and beauty, storms of fury and exasperation, a continual conflict of feelings, swinging almost hourly from extreme to extreme.

This very evening, for example. The wind had dropped. There was a fiery sunset and in this light the snow-covered mountains were all burned to opal and amethyst. They sparkled in well-water air, so pure, so clear, it bred a state of glory, of perfection. What a wonderful, marvellous place Greece was! There was nothing in the world to equal it.

And the Greeks after all, in spite of their follies, had splendid natural qualities. Even this local war, stupid and wasteful as it was, showed great vitality, coming at the end of four years of life at little above starvation level. If only, if only one didn't always have to qualify one's enthusiasm.

If only the Greeks were less mercurial, less volatile! Their quick intelligence always making them too divided to organize themselves, too opinionated to let anyone else do it for them. Their opinions change from moment to moment. They can do nothing together, have no feeling for the common good. Yet they have courage, dash and style, great patriotism, loyalty to their friends and a sharp business sense. But they are their own worst enemy. How, at the same time, can they be so devious, untrustworthy, have such an exaggerated sense of pride and no sense of honour?

This continual swing, these exaggerated antics of enthusiasm and laziness, leave us northerners, slow, steady stubborn in our ways, so exasperated that we really do not know how to deal with it. The Greek remains a mystery to anyone except a Greek — and even then they seem to infuriate one another. Only Pericles has ever been able to handle them and until they get another, I fear they are doomed to remain a little country — in spite of the seeds (or husks) of greatness that lie within them.

Independence Day

26 March.

Spring is almost here and the country is simply bursting with it, the scents, the colours, the immortal glory of an Athenian spring! And, wouldn't you know, it's all for me! I shall be forty-seven in a couple of weeks' time! Better still, old fossils like me get out at once. So this is probably my last letter to you from overseas. Hope you won't be disappointed when you see me in my Norfolk jacket and grey bags — the standard kit dished out to us when they throw us on to civvy street.

It's only now I'm going I can permit myself the nostalgia of dreaming of our little cottage down the lane and the bit of ground we planned to make into a garden — when peace came! Now it seems to be coming I can't quite believe it.

The Unit that I formed and brought to Greece was full of enthusiasm and high morale, but after we lost half of them, taken prisoner by ELAS and afterwards repatriated, it was never the same. The war is practically over. It is a sort of vacuum. Everybody wants to get home and get demobbed.

Here, in Greece, life is getting back to 'normal'. Athens is coming to life. The country went through a bad time, but now is full of hope and enthusiasm and I am glad to go while they are on a high. Greece in the spring seems to renew herself into the old country of the Gods.

This feeling seemed to come to a head on Independence Day, a national holiday more important to the country than any other — the day Greece finally threw off her long years of Turkish domination. One of the celebrations takes the form of a performance of Greek National Dancing and a display of their National Costumes.

Dancing is something absolutely central to life in Greece. Everybody, it seems, is born dancing. Every village has its own dances. The children are brought up to dance, on birthdays, at weddings, local feast days, national holidays, anything is an excuse to dance. And in the dancing you see all the best and most attractive sides of the Greek character, their gaiety, their spirit, their dash, exuberance and fire. Old customs, old costumes, old songs pour out of them and I suppose you see it at its best in the theatre performances put on in Athens.

Apparently there is a sort of Club which has taken on itself the care and preservation of old traditional costumes. The costumes are normally displayed in a Museum, but certain girls have the responsibility of looking after the care and preservation of selected costumes and are allowed to wear them at these annual shows. These costumes are very precious and it is considered a great honour to be allowed to take care of one.

So this evening the theatre was packed. It was the first celebration since the Hun occupation in 1940 and there was an electric tension and gaiety in the scene. It was a return to something at the very core of Greek life and there was a sort of joy in it I have never felt before. Dance followed dance, tune followed tune; the house was alert, applauding vigorously, calling for encores and again and again joining in themselves. I liked the Cretan dances best, for they, like their songs, have a wild intoxicating rhythm which swings you off your feet.

Then came the interval and the whole house went to mill around in the foyer. Most of the audience were wearing national costume and when to these were added all those who had been performing on stage and all the precious — and most beautiful — costumes as well, it was one of those moments that really took off and I felt there had never been anything like it — and maybe never would be again.

All the first half had been amateur, a showing off of national costumes by the daughters of old families, a sort of parade to admire and applaud and join in national tunes and dances that everybody could dance. But now it was the turn of the professionals, of those who specialized in the dances of certain villages or districts and the level of technical precision and style would be a performance to admire and applaud.

The girls came flooding back into the theatre overflowing into the aisles in wave after wave of colour and movement and laughter and gaiety that seemed to light up the whole auditorium and their enthusiasm for the dancers and their songs exploded, time after time, in waves of pleasure and applause. Just as strangers joined up in the tavernas when the old tunes got going and the whole place became one party, so here everything fused into a spontaneous outburst of national unity and joy. It was a contagious irrepressible gaiety that overflowed into the streets in the last light of evening, to find the Acropolis shining, the buildings floodlit and all Athens united in a moment of fulfilment and liberation. In such moments I felt there was no country in the world like Greece. Someday we should have to come back.